# beach house
## BRUNCH

**Also by Lei Shishak**

*Beach House Baking*

# beach house
## BRUNCH

100 Delicious Ways to Start Your Long Summer Days

## LEI SHISHAK

Photographs by Chau Vuong & Brent Lee

Skyhorse Publishing

Skyhorse Publishing books may be purchased in bulk at special discounts for sales promotion, corporate gifts, fund-raising, or educational purposes. Special editions can also be created to specifications. For details, contact the Special Sales Department, Skyhorse Publishing, 307 West 36th Street, 11th Floor, New York, NY 10018 or info@skyhorsepublishing.com.

Skyhorse® and Skyhorse Publishing® are registered trademarks of Skyhorse Publishing, Inc.®, a Delaware corporation.

Visit our website at www.skyhorsepublishing.com.

10 9 8 7 6 5 4 3 2 1

Library of Congress Cataloging-in-Publication Data is available on file.

Cover design by Laura Klynstra

Cover photo credit: neat

Print ISBN: 978-1-5107-0289-9

Ebook ISBN: 978-1-5107-0290-5

Printed in China

*BRUNCH (n): a late morning meal that is often shared with family and friends.*

# Contents

# Introduction

I've always believed food tastes better when shared with others, but we so often struggle to make the time to gather with friends to partake in it. These days, it's hard to find a moment when every friend is free and all can agree on a time and place to meet. This is followed, of course, by the ever-present dilemma of what to eat: paninis, pasta, salad, pancakes, seafood, steak, vegetarian—and is anyone bringing dessert?

Thanks to social media, sending a text once a month and following someone are enough to maintain a friendship. We all know deep down that this isn't enough and that gathering together is imperative. Brunch is the perfect remedy, and let me tell you why:

*The Food.* Something about the combination of breakfast and lunch is quite appealing. It's lighter than a full-scale breakfast and more decadent than a lunch. And the variety! You can go heavy on the sweet with dishes like my Bananas Foster Pancakes and Tiramisu Crepes, or go savory with dishes like my Italian Meats Quiche and Eggs Milanese.

*Let's Celebrate.* More often than not, brunch is a celebration. Be it a celebration of friendship, an engagement, a promotion, or a reunion. Brunch is the happiest meal come to life.

*Not Too Late, Not Too Early.* As any friend of mine will tell you, I'm not an early riser. So for my weekends, brunch is the most ideally timed meal for me. It's not too early that I can't sleep in, and it's not too late that I can't finish my errands afterward and make evening commitments.

*It's the Weekend.* Brunch is a sure sign that your weekend has arrived. It's time to relax, kick back, and eat some delicious food. However, brunch can be any day of the week. All that matters is that you're present and ready to eat.

The recipes in *Beach House Brunch* are appropriate for any home cook. They're straightforward and call for everyday ingredients. As you can imagine, as a professional baker, I'm in the kitchen a lot, both at home and at work. When hosting a brunch, I prepare dishes that allow me to spend more time with my guests instead of sweating over a hot stove. I hope you enjoy these dishes, which I often make for my beach house guests—which now includes you!

# Setting the Table

I'm often asked for easy tips for setting a table. With just a few simple steps, you can create the perfect table setting for your brunch. I've put together a checklist of items to consider that will help you along the way.

★ *Color:* The colors you use will depend on the type of brunch you are hosting—formal, casual, festive, morning, afternoon, etc. In general though, I recommend you choose up to two colors and stick to them. If you choose one color, try using different shades of that color. Once a decision is made, use those colors for select few items. For instance, if you choose to go with teal and coral, consider using a bold teal runner against a white tablecloth. Toss in some coral napkins and teal napkin rings. Then that's it—don't overdo it. Small pops of color go a long way. As with everything, there are of course exceptions. For instance, if you're hosting a fiesta themed brunch then numerous bold and bright colors are the way to go.

★ *Dishware:* Shallow bowls and platters are ideal so guests can see the food you worked so hard to prepare. I prefer solid color dishes that provide a nice backdrop for the food; patterned dishware detracts from the food. For salads, I recommend clear bowls.

★ *Glassware:* Invest in quality stemware and sturdy drinking glasses. If your dishwasher is like mine, soap spots on glassware are the norm. Take the time the night before to polish your glassware with a soft cloth. It'll be one less thing you have to worry about the next day.

★ *Plates:* Choose medium to large plates for your guests to use. You don't want them to feel restricted in any way; they should feel free to eat as much as they want. If you're using disposable plates, choose sturdy ones with a lip. Oh, and it's perfectly fine to mix and match plate designs. They're great conversation starters.

★ *Utensils:* Even if you choose to use disposable plates, I always prefer to use silverware. Make sure to polish them the night before, as this is a task that always seems to be overlooked on the day of the brunch. During the meal, I never fail to somehow exchange, misplace, or misuse the utensils, so I always keep a canning jar full of extra utensils on the table just in case.

★ *Flowers:* Flowers are an easy way to make your brunch special, but you have to use them wisely. Most flower centerpieces prevent guests from seeing each other and can limit conversation. They often get knocked over during the meal and deter guests from sampling dishes blocked from their sight or out of their reach. While they do work well on a brunch buffet table as a backdrop, if you're setting a dining table, I recommend using short, clear glasses filled with blooms, pebbles, and water. Another great way to incorporate flowers into your brunch is to set single stem blooms on each plate setting.

★ *Candles:* I like tall, skinny candles for brunch buffet tables, but make sure to place them in the back behind the food so they aren't disturbed. Votive candles on a dining table are particularly lovely for a late autumn brunch. Choose lightly scented or unscented candles if you plan to place them near food.

★ *Tablecloth and Napkins:* Unless you have a table whose artistic design must be seen by all or a varnished wood table, I typically recommend using tablecloths. Aside from protecting your dining table, a tablecloth dresses up the occasion and buffs any noise caused by plates and glasses clanging around the table. Cloth napkins are the way to go for brunch. I typically like less fuss, but there's something about cloth napkins for brunch that make your guests feel special.

★ *Music:* Playing soft music in the background is always a nice touch, especially once people start eating. Everyone appreciates a little background noise.

Large Dice

Medium Dice

Brunoise

Coins

Julienne

Small Dice

Mince

Chiffonade

# Basic Knife Cuts

One of the first things I learned in culinary school is the basic knife cuts used when cooking. Many of these knife cuts are mentioned throughout this book and should be followed in order to achieve the best recipe results. While these cuts may seem a bit elementary, it is really important to make them a part of your set of kitchen skills.

*Large dice* = ¾-inch cube

*Medium dice* = ½-inch cube

*Small dice* = ¼-inch cube

*Brunoise* = $\frac{1}{8}$-inch cube

*Mince* = very fine pieces, smaller than *Fine Brunoise*

*Coins* = sliced into coin-shapes

*Julienne* = $\frac{1}{8}$ × $\frac{1}{8}$ × 2½-inch strips

*Chiffonade* = thin shreds of leafy vegetables and herbs, prepared by stacking and rolling up the leaves and slicing very thin

*Prosecco and Guava Bellini*

# Beverages

Drinking beverages is a great way to start any meal, especially brunch. Many brunch lovers even feel that the beverages served are more important than the food. No matter on which side of that argument you fall, these drink recipes will allow you to beautifully represent the liquid side of brunch.

Countless brunch beverages exist, so what follows is a sampling of some classics and variations on others. I've shared a great recipe for Infused Water that I'm confident is more delicious than you expect, and I've used roasted beets in my Bloody Mary, which adds a touch of sweetness and a gorgeous red hue that always takes guests by surprise. Need a beverage for a celebration? Try my Guava Bellini, a refreshing variation on the classic Italian beverage.

| | |
|---|---|
| **Roasted Beet Bloody Mary** | **Strawberry Smoothie** |
| 11 | 21 |
| **Cafe Au Lait D'almande** | **Prosecco and Guava Bellini** |
| 13 | 21 |
| **Classic Mimosa** | **Gin Fizz** |
| 15 | 23 |
| **Vanilla Bean French Press Coffee** | **Jasmine Lime Iced Tea** |
| 15 | 24 |
| **Infused Water** | **White Cocoa with Cinnamon Marshmallows** |
| 17 | 26 |
| **Slow Cooker Mulled Cider** | |
| 17 | |

# Roasted Beet Bloody Mary

## Makes 4 servings

*By adding roasted beets to my Bloody Mary, I've achieved a brunch cocktail with an earthy sweetness and gorgeous shade of red. Be sure to select beets that are firm and have noticeable weight to them.*

Preheat oven to 375°F and place a sheet tray on the middle rack.

Place the beets and olive oil in a large bowl and toss to coat. Wrap each beet in aluminum foil, place on the sheet tray, and roast until cooked through, about an hour. Insert a sharp paring knife into the beet centers to check for doneness. You should be able to insert and remove knife without any resistance. Let beets cool for 30 minutes. Peel and cut beets into small wedges. Place in a blender or food processor, and purée until smooth.

In a large pitcher, whisk together 2 cups of the puréed beets and the remaining ingredients. Pour into mason jars filled with ice cubes and garnish with celery stalks, lemon wedges, and pickles.

*Other fun garnishes include pickled carrots, chilled cooked shrimp, pepper jack cheese cubes, and cucumber slices.*

3 medium beets, scrubbed, leaves trimmed

¼ cup olive oil

3 cups tomato juice

1 cup filtered water

½ cup vodka

4 teaspoons celery salt

4 teaspoons Worcestershire

4 teaspoons fresh lemon juice

4 dashes tabasco sauce

2 tablespoons pickle juice

2 teaspoons horseradish cream

½ teaspoon salt

celery stalks, lemon wedges, and pickles for garnish

# Cafe Au Lait D'almande

*This is a simple way to make coffee a bit more interesting. Your lactose-sensitive guests will be especially appreciative of it, too. This recipe calls for homemade almond milk which requires you to soak the almonds overnight. If you're short on time, store-bought almond milk is a fine option. You'll need a mesh strainer and cheese cloth for this one.*

1 cup whole almonds

2 cups water, plus more for soaking

4 cups fresh brewed dark roast coffee

2 tablespoons sugar

*The night before:*
Place the almonds in a small bowl and cover completely with water to about an inch high. Cover bowl with a dish towel and let sit on the counter overnight. The almonds will soak up the water and plump overnight.

*The next day:*
Drain the almonds in a colander and rinse well with cool running water. Transfer the almonds to a blender and add 2 cups water. Blend on high until almonds are broken down to a fine meal, about 2 minutes. The water will turn to milky white. Place the strainer over a bowl or bain-marie. Line the strainer with a large piece of cheese cloth. Pour the almond milk through the cheese cloth. Gather the cloth and squeeze out as much milk from the almond meal as possible. You should end up with about 2 cups of almond milk. Discard cloth and set aside milk while you brew the coffee.

When the coffee is ready, warm the almond milk and sugar in a small pot over medium heat. The milk will thicken as it warms. Combine coffee and warm almond milk. Serve immediately.

Vanilla Bean French Press Coffee

# Classic Mimosa

*I've found that Spanish Cava is an affordable and tasty sparkling wine that makes outstanding mimosas. Paired with freshly squeezed orange juice, an equal proportion of Cava is the way to go.*

Fill six champagne flutes halfway with the Cava.

Top with orange juice. Serve immediately.

1 (750 mL) bottle Cava, well chilled

3 cups (about 10–12 oranges) fresh squeezed orange juice, well chilled

*I prefer Brut Cava which is dry, not sweet.*

# Vanilla Bean French Press Coffee

*This artisan coffee is so much better than the flavored ones found in grocery stores—those always taste so artificial and overly sweet to me. Stick to this recipe and you, too, will never go back. You'll need a grinder and a coffee press for this one.*

Coarsely grind the coffee beans. (I have a small hand-held grinder and pulse it twice for 3 seconds each time. You want the grounds to resemble steel-cut oats.) Add the grounds and the split vanilla bean to the coffee press.

Add the water to a pot and bring to a boil over high heat. Pour the water slowly over the grounds and bean. Let sit for 30 seconds then gently stir the grounds with a spoon for a few seconds. Place the plunger on top and let soak for 6 minutes. Slowly depress plunger, pour into coffee mugs, and enjoy immediately.

1 cup whole coffee beans, medium roast

1-inch vanilla bean, split

4¼ cups filtered water

*Infused Water*

# INFUSED WATER

MAKES 1 GALLON

*This is a great way to make sure your guests stay hydrated during their meal (especially if they're partaking in bottomless cocktails). Guests will find themselves refilling their glasses with this surprisingly delicious water.*

Add the raspberries, orange slices, mint, and lime slices to your pitcher. Slowly pour the water over and keep chilled in the refrigerator until serving time. Chill the water at least 10 minutes before serving to allow sufficient infusion.

1 (4-ounce) pack raspberries

3 cross-sectional slices of an orange

2 mint sprigs

1 lime, sliced

1 gallon filtered water, chilled

# SLOW COOKER MULLED CIDER

MAKES ½ GALLON

*Nothing warms your guests on a cool day better than this soothing cider. Use of a slow cooker makes this recipe easy to make, and its long simmering time allows the flavors of citrus and spice to shine through.*

Add the apple cider and sugar to your slow cooker. Stir to dissolve sugar.

Insert the cloves into the flesh of the apple and orange halves. Place the fruit flesh-side down in the cider. Add the remaining ingredients. Cook on high for 2 hours. Strain and serve warm.

½ gallon apple cider

½ cup sugar

1 large Fuji apple, halved with skin on

1 large Navel orange, halved with skin on

10 cloves

5 cardamom pods

2 strips lemon zest

1 (2-inch) cinnamon stick

1 large bay leaf

1 black tea bag (I like Bigelow's Constant Comment)

*Slow Cooker Mulled Cider*

*Strawberry Smoothie*

# STRAWBERRY SMOOTHIE

## MAKES 4 SERVINGS

*This energizing smoothie is made with lots of fresh strawberries and protein-packed yogurt. It's a quick and yummy way for your guests to cool off and fill up.*

24 ounces strawberries, hulled and halved

2 cups Greek strained yogurt (I prefer Fage)

½ cup sugar

1 tablespoon fresh lime juice

ice cubes

Combine the strawberries, yogurt, sugar, and lime juice in a blender. Pulse until combined. Add water to thin if desired. Serve over ice.

*Because it is strained of liquid whey, Greek yogurt has a wonderfully thick texture and tangy flavor that makes it ideal for smoothies. Additionally, this creamy yogurt has a higher protein, lower carb, and lower sodium content than regular yogurt.*

# PROSECCO AND GUAVA BELLINI

## MAKES 5 SERVINGS

*This classic beverage was first seen in Venice, Italy, at the famed Harry's Bar. Owner Giuseppe Cipriani created the drink in the 1940s, inspired by his love of white peaches and the pink glow of a painting by fifteenth-century Venetian painter Giovanni Bellini. My version uses guava in lieu of peach yet still retains the beautiful pink hue of the original. I prefer my bellini chilled so I like to add a few extra ice cubes on really sunny days.*

1¼ cups Kern's guava nectar, well chilled

1 (750mL) bottle Prosecco, well chilled

ice cubes, if desired

*I prefer Ecco Domani Prosecco.*

Pour ¼ cup of nectar into each champagne flute. Top off each flute with Prosecco. Add ice cubes, if desired. Cheers!

# GIN FIZZ

*My favorite cocktail is Hendricks and Tonic. When I'm in the mood for something a little sweeter, I treat my guests to a Gin Fizz with solid undertones of gin and a sweet playfulness.*

Combine gin, lemon juice, and powdered sugar in shaker. Shake vigorously and divide evenly into four highball glasses filled with ice. Top each glass with the club soda and garnish with fresh mint or lemon slices.

1 cup Hendrick's gin

½ cup fresh lemon juice

4 teaspoons powdered sugar

ice cubes

2 cups club soda

mint sprigs or lemon slices for garnishing

# JASMINE LIME ICED TEA

MAKES 4 SERVINGS

4 cups filtered water

2 limes, thinly sliced

2 tablespoons orange blossom honey

6 jasmine green tea bags

2 trays of ice plus more for serving

*I recommend Numi Jasmine Green Organic Tea.*

*Jasmine green tea is a mild and aromatic tea full of antioxidants. When flavored with lime and served chilled, it's a refreshing beverage your guests will savor and recall for days to come.*

In a medium pot over high heat, bring water and 4 lime slices to just a boil. Remove from heat and gently stir in the honey and tea bags. Cover and let steep for 5 minutes.

Fill a pitcher with 2 trays of ice and the remaining lime slices. Strain tea into pitcher. Serve over additional ice.

# WHITE COCOA
# WITH CINNAMON MARSHMALLOWS

MAKES 4 SERVINGS

*Cinnamon Marshmallows:*

4 teaspoons gelatin

½ cup water

1 cup sugar

2 tablespoons corn syrup

1 large egg white

1 teaspoon ground cinnamon

1 teaspoon vanilla extract

2 cups powdered sugar, for coating

*White Cocoa:*

1 cup heavy cream

1 cup white chocolate, chopped

3 cups whole milk

pinch of salt

*This sweet white chocolate beverage is a nice change from traditional hot cocoa. It's fun to make something that your guests think they know and switch up the ingredients to surprise them. This drink is perfect for serving at holiday brunches with a candy cane garnish.*

*Make cinnamon marshmallows:*

Grease an 8-inch square pan and then coat it with powdered sugar. Set aside. Bloom the gelatin in ¼ cup of the water in a mixing bowl and set aside. Add the remaining water to a small pot, along with the sugar and corn syrup. Place pot over high heat and cook to 240°F. Immediately pour the sugar syrup over the gelatin and whip on high speed until fluffy and white, about 4 minutes. In a separate bowl, whisk the egg white, cinnamon, and vanilla until aerated and foamy. Add to the mixer and whip on medium speed to incorporate the egg white. Immediately transfer the marshmallow to the prepared pan with a greased spatula. Smooth out the top and place in refrigerator to set up, about 30 minutes.

Run a knife around the pan edges and peel out the marshmallow. Cut into squares, transfer to a large bowl filled with powdered sugar, and toss to coat. Shake off excess powdered sugar and store marshmallows in an airtight container at room temperature.

*Make white cocoa:*

Add the cream to a medium pot and bring to a boil over high heat. Remove from heat and add the white chocolate. Let the chocolate sit submerged for 30 seconds. Whisk until ganache is smooth. Place the ganache over low heat while simultaneously warming the milk in the microwave. Then whisk the milk into the ganache. Stir in the salt. Portion into mugs and top with the cinnamon marshmallows.

# Fruit Reconsidered

Fruit is delicious as is but sometimes it's nice to mix things up a bit. Serving fruit in unique ways opens our eyes to the possibilities of flavor combinations we don't normally consider. Grapefruit and tarragon, pineapple and anise, orange and cilantro—these are just some of the combinations that you'll find this chapter. In my opinion, they all make wonderful side dishes before, after, or during a meal.

**White Nectarines in Serrano Chili, Honey, and Ginger**

31

**Watermelon Pops**

31

**Broiled Grapefruit with Brown Sugar and Tarragon**

32

**Strawberries, Cabernet, and Black Pepper**

34

**Orange, Cilantro, Cloves, and Brown Sugar**

37

**Marsala Poached Pears, Blue Cheese, and Honey**

38

**Grilled Pineapple with Cinnamon and Anise**

41

**Cantaloupe, Chili, and Lime**

42

*Watermelon Pops*

# White Nectarines in Serrano Chili, Honey, and Ginger

Makes 8 servings

*The heat in this dish sneaks up on you moments after the first bite. The warm honey brings out sweetness while the ginger and chili add an unexpected dimension. Serve it with a scoop of vanilla ice cream when you're looking for a unique summer dessert.*

8 ripe white nectarines, chilled

2 cups water

1 cup orange blossom honey

4-inch piece of fresh ginger, peeled and sliced into coins

2 serrano chilis, seeded and sliced lengthwise into ¼-inch thick strips

Wash nectarines well and slice into quarters. Discard pits. Place in a large bowl and set aside.

Combine remaining ingredients in a pot and bring to a boil over high heat. Let boil for 3 minutes then pour over the nectarines and stir to coat. Let sit for 5 minutes then strain and serve.

# Watermelon Pops

Yields 4–6 servings

*This is a fun way to serve watermelon to your guests. Instead of serving typical wedges, liven up your brunch by carving this summertime staple into pops. I'm a big fan of personal watermelons; they're so much easier to cut. You'll need a cutting board and a sharp knife for this one.*

1 personal watermelon, chilled

Wash and dry the watermelon. On a secure cutting board, use a sharp knife to slice the fruit in half. Working with one half at a time (cut-side down), make 1-inch-thick slices in one direction, followed by the other direction to form 1-inch square pops.

*If hosting an outdoor brunch, keep the pops chilled by arranging them over ice.*

# BROILED GRAPEFRUIT
## WITH BROWN SUGAR AND TARRAGON

2 pink grapefruits,
halved

¼ cup light brown sugar

¼ teaspoon balsamic
vinegar

10 tarragon leaves,
ripped into small
pieces

*This is a great first-course dish to serve at brunch. Guests are always surprised at how well tarragon pairs with grapefruit and how they work together to awaken the palate. Broiling grapefruit brings out its juices and allows the brown sugar to melt and seep into the tangy fruit below.*

Turn broiler to high. Line a sheet tray with aluminum foil. Place the grapefruit halves on it and set aside.

Combine the brown sugar, balsamic, and tarragon leaves in a small bowl. Spread the mixture onto the grapefruit halves. Broil in oven for 3 minutes or until sugar has melted. Serve warm.

# Strawberries, Cabernet, and Black Pepper

MAKES 4 SERVINGS

1 pound strawberries, chilled

½ cup cabernet sauvignon

¼ cup sugar

freshly ground pepper

*We've all made the unfortunate mistake of buying strawberries and bringing them home only to discover they lack flavor. This is a good way to dress up those strawberries and turn them into something delicious.*

Clean and dry the strawberries well. Slice them in half and place in a large zip top bag.

In a small pot, warm the cabernet and sugar over high heat until sugar is completely dissolved. Remove from heat and slowly pour over the strawberries. Seal the bag well, making sure to get out all the air. Lay flat in refrigerator for 10 minutes.

Drain strawberries in colander. Arrange on plate and place in refrigerator to chill. Top with freshly ground pepper before serving.

# Orange, Cilantro, Cloves, and Brown Sugar

*This flavor pairing of orange and cilantro is delightfully bright thanks to the loud floral notes of cilantro and the piercing citrus notes of orange.*

Warm a small nonstick sauté pan over medium heat. Add the almonds and 1 tablespoon brown sugar and stir continuously as sugar caramelizes and almonds toast, about 3 to 4 minutes. Transfer to a piece of aluminum foil to cool.

In a small pot over high heat, bring the water and raisins to a boil for 30 seconds. Remove from heat, cover, and let sit for 5 minutes to rehydrate raisins. Strain and set aside.

Combine the remaining brown sugar and ground cloves in a large bowl. Cut the ends of the oranges off and discard. Stand up the oranges on a cut side and slice off the rind as close to the flesh as possible. Cut ½-inch-thick cross-sectional slices and then cut each slice into quarters. Add the orange wedges to the brown sugar mixture and toss to coat. Add the cilantro and almonds and mix well. Sweeten with more brown sugar if needed. Serve immediately.

¼ cup sliced almonds

2 tablespoons light brown sugar

1 cup warm water

¼ cup dark raisins

5 cloves, ground

3 large navel oranges, chilled

⅓ cup chopped cilantro

# MARSALA POACHED PEARS, BLUE CHEESE, AND HONEY

## MAKES 4 SERVINGS

½ cup walnuts, finely chopped

2 cups sweet marsala

½ cup sugar

2 tablespoons honey

2 tablespoons unsalted butter

2 ripe Bosc pears, peeled, halved, and center cored

½ cup blue cheese

salt for sprinkling

*Warm pears poached in sweet marsala are incredibly light and divine. In this recipe, the sharp tang of blue cheese is mellowed by the subtly sweet pear and finished with the woody flavor of marsala. Turn this dish into an entrée by serving the pears atop an arugula salad.*

Toast the chopped walnuts in a small sauté pan over high heat. Agitate them continuously until golden brown and fragrant, about 3 minutes. Transfer nuts to a plate and place in the refrigerator to cool.

Bring marsala, sugar, honey, and butter to a boil over high heat. Reduce heat and bring to a simmer. Add pears cut-side down, cover pot, and cook. Flip pears over halfway through cooking. Cook until fruit is fork tender, about 25 minutes. Transfer pears to a platter and continue cooking sauce, uncovered, until thickened, about 15 minutes. Remove from heat.

Form four balls of blue cheese with your hands and roll them in the toasted walnuts. Top the pears with cheese balls and drizzle with the marsala syrup. Sprinkle with a little salt. Serve immediately.

# GRILLED PINEAPPLE
## WITH CINNAMON AND ANISE

*The delicious grilled flavors of brown sugar, cinnamon, vanilla, and anise really shine through in this preparation of pineapple. As a dessert, this dish pairs wonderfully with coconut gelato. As a savory dish, try layering the pineapple in grilled cheese and bacon sandwiches.*

peanut or canola oil

½ teaspoon anise seeds

1 cup light brown sugar

1 teaspoon ground cinnamon

1 teaspoon pure vanilla extract

1 ripe pineapple

Preheat your outdoor grill to medium high and lightly oil the grate.

Finely grind the anise seeds in a mortar and pestle. Add to a large zip top bag along with the brown sugar, cinnamon, and vanilla. Shake to combine.

Peel, core, and cut the pineapple into ½-inch cross-sectional slices. Place them in the zip top bag and shake to coat. Cook pineapple on grill until caramelized and heated through, about 3 to 4 minutes per side.

# CANTALOUPE, CHILI, AND LIME

MAKES 4 SERVINGS

1 ripe cantaloupe, chilled

1 teaspoon chili powder

1 teaspoon salt

1 lime

*I prefer using Tuscan cantaloupes because they have a vibrant orange flesh, sweet flavor, and rich aroma.*

*This refreshing preparation of cantaloupe is inspired by the fruit carts that line the streets of Los Angeles. If you don't love cantaloupe, choose a melon that yields to slight pressure and has a sweet musky scent.*

Using a sharp chef's knife and a cutting board, slice off both ends of the cantaloupe. Stand the melon up on a cut side and slice off the rind as close to the flesh as possible. Slice the melon in half (either way works) and remove the seeds. Working with one half at a time, use a melon baller to scoop out the fruit. Place the melon balls in a large bowl.

Stir together the chili powder, salt, and zest of 1 lime in a small bowl. Sprinkle over the melon balls. Squeeze the juice of the lime on top and toss lightly until fruit is evenly coated. Serve immediately.

Jumbo Morning Glory Muffins

# Sweet Pastries

Brunch is a great reason to forego the diet, brush off the stand mixer, and make something ooey gooey and delicious. After all, only at brunch is it completely acceptable to have something sweet as a main course.

A basket of freshly baked pastries easily stands out when placed on a table full of savory food. If the pastries are as tasty as they should be, those sweets will be remembered long after the brunch is over. As an added bonus, the aroma of fresh baking will create just the right setting for the wonderful meal to come.

Some of my favorites in this chapter include Easy Apple Turnovers, Croissants, and Nutella Pop Tarts. Many of the pastries can be prepped the night before and baked in the morning, leaving you with sweet dreams of Danish pastries and croissants all night long.

# EASY APPLE TURNOVERS

MAKES ABOUT 10 TURNOVERS

*So often sweets are a last-minute thought when planning a brunch. (Yes, even for me sometimes!) These easy turnovers will add something sweet to your brunch with plenty of time to spare.*

*Make filling:*
Peel, core, and cut apples into ¼-inch cubes. Place in a medium pot with the remaining ingredients and bring to a boil over medium-high heat. Continue to cook, uncovered, until water dries up, about 6 to 8 minutes, stirring occasionally. Transfer the apple mixture to a bowl and place in freezer to cool.

*Make turnovers:*
Preheat oven to 375°F. Line two sheet trays with aluminum foil and set aside.

Unroll the Filo dough, separate the top sheet, place on a flat clean counter, and brush it with some melted butter. Sprinkle with a little sugar and fold the sheet in half lengthwise. Brush with some more melted butter and sugar. Place a heaping tablespoon of the apple filling in the bottom right (or left) corner of the dough and then roll up in the form of a triangle. Place on the prepared sheet tray and brush with butter. Repeat this step with the remaining Filo sheets until you use up all the filling.

Bake for 10 minutes. Rotate. Bake 5 minutes more. Let cool at least 5 minutes before sprinkling with powdered sugar and serving.

*Leftovers should be stored in a ziptop bag for up to a week in the freezer and reheated in a 400°F oven for 10 minutes.*

Filling:

2 medium (about 12 ounces) Fuji apples

⅓ cup water

1½ tablespoons sugar

1 tablespoon unsalted butter

¼ teaspoon ground cinnamon

⅛ teaspoon ground nutmeg

Turnovers:

1 roll Filo dough, thawed in refrigerator

¼ cup unsalted butter, melted

¼ cup sugar

powdered sugar, for garnish

# BLACKBERRY STREUSEL COFFEE CAKE

MAKES ONE 10-INCH TUBE CAKE

Filling:
1¼ cups (6 ounces) blackberries
2 tablespoons sugar
½ teaspoon ground cinnamon

Cake:
1 cup unsalted butter, soft
1½ cups sugar
2 large eggs
½ teaspoon pure vanilla extract
2¼ cups all-purpose flour
1 teaspoon baking powder
½ teaspoon baking soda
⅛ teaspoon salt
1 cup sour cream

Streusel:
½ cup all-purpose flour
⅓ cup light brown sugar
2 tablespoons unsalted butter, melted
½ teaspoon ground cinnamon

*Coffee cake at brunch just feels right. I usually make this the day before so it's ready to serve in the morning with coffee. Macerating the blackberries before adding to the batter brings out the sweet berry juices and flavor.*

*Make filling:*
Slice the blackberries in half and toss them in a small bowl with the sugar and cinnamon. Set aside to macerate.

*Make cake:*
Preheat oven to 350°F. Grease a 10-inch tube pan generously with cooking spray and set aside.

In a mixer fitted with the paddle attachment, cream the butter and sugar on medium speed until light and fluffy, about 2 minutes. Add the eggs and vanilla and mix well. In a separate bowl, whisk together the dry ingredients and add to the mixer alternately with the sour cream on low speed. Spread two-thirds of the batter into the prepared pan. Spoon the blackberries evenly over the batter. Top with remaining batter, spreading it out to cover the blackberries completely.

*Make streusel:*
In a small bowl, combine all the streusel ingredients and mix well with your hand until mixture resembles sand. Sprinkle evenly over top of batter.

Bake for 70 minutes or until an inserted toothpick comes out clean. Remove from oven and let sit for at least 1 hour before inverting. Place right-side up onto serving plate and garnish with powdered sugar.

# CROISSANTS

*When it comes to making croissants, I always use Plugra butter. Its higher fat content yields a flaky and tender multi-layered pastry. These croissants are wonderful alone or as part of an egg sandwich. Don't be tempted to shorten the chilling time of the dough; this is one of the most important steps to achieving beautiful, even layers.*

**Croissants:**

1¼ cups whole milk, lukewarm

5 tablespoons sugar

1 package active dry yeast

4 cups all-purpose flour

10 ounces Plugra salted butter, cold and cubed

*Make croissants:*

Combine ¼ cup of the milk, 1 tablespoon of the sugar, and the yeast in a small bowl. Let sit for 10 minutes to activate yeast.

Add the flour and remaining sugar to a mixing bowl fitted with the hook attachment. With the mixer on low speed, add the remaining milk and yeast mixture. Mix until the dough comes together, about 1 minute.

With the mixer running on medium speed, gradually add the cold, cubed Plugra and continue mixing until butter is incorporated, about 3 minutes. You may have to scrape the bowl occasionally to evenly distribute the butter. Transfer dough to plastic wrap. Flatten to a rectangle and wrap well. Place in refrigerator for 30 to 40 minutes until well chilled.

**Egg Wash:**

1 large egg

1 tablespoon water

¼ cup corn syrup

On a lightly floured surface, roll out the dough into a ½-inch-thick rectangle. Fold the left third of the dough into the center. Brush off any flour from the dough. Fold the right third over the left flap. Rotate dough 90° and then roll out dough again to a ½-inch-thick rectangle and repeat folding process. Wrap dough well and place in refrigerator for 30 minutes.

Repeat the rolling and folding process in the previous step. Chill dough for 30 minutes. Line a sheet tray with parchment paper or aluminum foil and set aside.

*Continued on page 52*

Remove dough from refrigerator and divide the dough in half. Roll out each half on a lightly floured surface to make two ¼-inch-thick rectangles (about 13 × 9 inches each). Using a pizza cutter or sharp knife, cut each rectangle in half lengthwise. Then cut each strip diagonally to form two long, skinny triangles, about 4½ inches wide at the base. You will end up with eight triangular strips.

Starting at the base of the triangle, roll up the dough toward the tip of the triangle, creating a crescent shape. Transfer croissants to the prepared tray. Cover with a dish towel and let rise in a warm place until doubled in size, about 1 hour.

*Make egg wash:*
Preheat oven to 400°F. Whisk the egg and water together in a small bowl. Pour the corn syrup into a separate small bowl. Right before baking, brush the egg wash onto the croissants with a pastry brush. Bake croissants for 20 minutes. Remove from oven and brush the croissants with corn syrup. Let cool for 10 minutes before serving. These are best served the day they're made.

---

*After you shape the croissants, you can freeze them in a zip top bag for up to four months. When you want to bake them, simply place the frozen croissants on a foil-lined sheet tray, cover with a dish towel, and let rise at room temperature until doubled in size. Bake according to directions.*

# Jumbo Morning Glory Muffins

*A glorious baked treat to have at your brunches, these muffins are moist, hearty, and healthy with a wonderful mix of flavors including cinnamon, earthy walnuts, sweet carrots, and tangy pineapple.*

Preheat oven to 350°F. Place liners in a jumbo muffin pan and set pan aside.

In a large bowl, whisk together the flour, sugar, baking soda, cinnamon, and salt. Stir in the carrots, raisins, coconut, and walnuts. Set aside.

In another large bowl, whisk together the eggs, oil, pineapple, and shredded apple. Add the dry ingredients and mix with a rubber spatula until incorporated.

Fill muffin liners three-quarters full. Sprinkle each muffin with a teaspoon of sunflower seeds. Bake for 28 to 30 minutes or until centers bounce back when pressed.

2 cups all-purpose flour

1¼ cups sugar

1 teaspoon baking soda

1 teaspoon ground cinnamon

½ teaspoon salt

1 cup grated carrots

¾ cup dark raisins

½ cup sweetened coconut, shredded

½ cup walnuts, finely chopped

3 large eggs

¾ cup vegetable oil

½ cup crushed pineapple, drained

1 medium Fuji apple, peeled and shredded

10 teaspoons raw sunflower seeds

# Honey Oat Bran Muffins

## Honey Sauce:
3 tablespoons salted butter
3 tablespoons sugar
3 tablespoons brown sugar
3 tablespoons honey
2 tablespoons water

## Muffins:
1 cup whole wheat flour
1 cup oat bran
¼ cup light brown sugar
1 teaspoon baking powder
1 teaspoon baking soda
¼ teaspoon salt
½ cup dark raisins
2 large egg whites
1 cup whole milk
½ cup water
¼ cup molasses
2 tablespoons canola oil

*These super moist muffins taste so amazing, you forget how good they are for you. I often serve them sliced in half, toasted, and topped with butter.*

Preheat oven to 325°F. Coat a 12-cup muffin pan with cooking spray.

*Make honey sauce:*
In a small pot, warm all the ingredients over medium heat and stir until sugars dissolve. Add 2 teaspoons of the honey sauce to each muffin cup. Set aside.

*Make muffins:*
In a large bowl, whisk together the flour, oat bran, brown sugar, baking powder, baking soda, salt, and raisins. Make a well in the center and add the egg whites, milk, water, molasses, and oil. Whisk until combined.

Use a large ice cream scoop or ladle to portion the batter to just below the rim of each muffin cup. While portioning, stir the muffin batter in the bowl occasionally to evenly distribute the raisins. Bake muffins for 18 minutes or until centers are firm when pressed. Remove from oven and let sit for a few minutes before inverting onto a foil-lined sheet tray. Let muffins cool for 10 minutes. Place them in muffin liners for serving.

*You can bake these cupcakes in muffin liners if you prefer a quick cleanup. You'll just need to bake the muffins in the oven for about 5 minutes longer.*

# APRICOT SCONES

## MAKES 8 SCONES

2¼ cups all-purpose flour

½ cup dried apricots, finely chopped

⅓ cup sugar, plus more for sprinkling

1 tablespoon baking powder

2 teaspoons grated fresh ginger

1 teaspoon orange zest

½ teaspoon salt

1½ sticks (6 ounces) unsalted butter, cold and cubed

½ cup half-and-half, plus more for brushing

1 teaspoon pure vanilla extract

*The addition of orange zest and fresh ginger gives this buttery scone a nice bright pop of flavor. They're excellent served with sausages and dabs of honey butter. Before guests arrive, I often sneak away to a quiet corner of my patio to enjoy a cup of coffee with these delicious morning sweets.*

Preheat oven to 375°F. Line a sheet tray with aluminum foil and set aside.

In a mixing bowl with the paddle attachment, mix together the flour, apricots, sugar, baking powder, grated ginger, orange zest, and salt. Add the butter and mix on low speed until pea-sized chunks of butter remain. Add the half-and-half and vanilla. Mix on low speed just until dough comes together. Transfer dough to a floured table and shape into a flat, rectangular strip about 16 inches long and 2½ inches wide. Using a sharp knife, cut into eight squares and arrange on prepared tray.

Brush scones with some half-and-half. Generously sprinkle each with sugar. Bake for 20 minutes or until centers are firm when pressed. Let cool for 10 minutes before serving.

# DATE BARS

MAKES ONE 13 × 9-INCH PAN

*These scrumptious bars have a buttery cinnamon crust with a gentle bite and a light, sugary oat topping. In the middle of all this yumminess is a delicious date filling spiked with orange zest and dotted with nuts and coconut. I love to send any extras home with my guests.*

Grease a 13 × 9-inch baking pan with cooking spray. Preheat oven to 400°F.

*Make filling:*
Combine dates, sugar, and water in a medium pot and cook over medium-high heat, stirring occasionally until thickened, about 10 minutes. Remove from heat and stir in the coconut, nuts, rum, and zest. Set aside to cool.

*Make crust:*
Cream butter and brown sugar in a mixing bowl fitted with the paddle attachment for 1 minute on medium speed. Add the remaining ingredients and mix on low speed until combined. Resulting mixture will be crumbly.

Spread 2½ cups of the oat mixture into the prepared pan. Firmly pat down the oat mixture and then spread the date mixture on top. Sprinkle the remaining oat mixture on top and gently press it down. You want it to remain somewhat crumbly.

Bake for 25 minutes until lightly browned on top. Let cool completely before cutting.

*Filling:*

3 cups pitted dates, chopped

¼ cup sugar

1½ cups water

¼ cup sweetened coconut flakes

¼ cup walnuts or pecans, finely chopped

1 tablespoon dark rum (I prefer Appleton)

1 teaspoon orange zest

*Crust:*

½ cup unsalted butter, soft

1 cup dark brown sugar

1½ cups all-purpose flour

1½ cups rolled oats

1 teaspoon orange zest

¾ teaspoon salt

½ teaspoon baking soda

¼ teaspoon ground cinnamon

# Pecan Sweet Bread

MAKES ONE 10-INCH SPRINGFORM PAN

### Dough:

2¼ teaspoons active dry yeast

¼ cup warm water

½ teaspoon sugar

½ cup whole milk, warm

½ cup fresh orange juice

½ cup sugar

½ cup ricotta cheese

1 teaspoon orange zest

½ teaspoon salt

1 large egg

4 cups all-purpose flour

### Pecan Topping:

¼ cup pecans, finely chopped

¼ cup sugar

½ teaspoon orange zest

2 tablespoons unsalted butter, melted

*I found this bread recipe in an old box of saved recipes, but I have no idea where it came from. I added the pecan sugar topping to make it sweeter and prettier. It has a chewy texture and pairs well with coffee, especially my Café au Lait D'Almande (see page 13).*

In a small bowl, dissolve the yeast in the warm water and sugar. Let stand for 5 minutes until bubbly. Meanwhile, combine the warm milk, orange juice, sugar, ricotta cheese, orange zest, salt, and egg in a mixing bowl fitted with the dough attachment. Add the yeast mixture and mix on low speed for 1 minute. Beat in the flour, 1 cup at a time, until the dough comes together. Transfer the dough to a greased bowl. Cover with a dish towel and let rise in a warm place until doubled, about 1½ hours.

While the dough is rising, grease a 10-inch springform pan and set aside. In a medium bowl, combine the chopped pecans, sugar, and orange zest.

After dough has risen, punch down dough and turn out onto a lightly floured surface. Divide dough into three equal pieces and roll each piece into a 20-inch long rope. Braid the ropes together. Starting in the center of the prepared pan, coil the dough and tuck the end under the dough. Cover with a dish towel and let rise in a warm place until doubled, about 30 minutes.

Preheat oven to 425°F. Brush the dough with the melted butter and sprinkle the top with the pecan sugar mixture. Bake until golden brown and the center bounces back when pressed, about 25 to 30 minutes. Let cool completely before serving.

# DONUTS

2 tablespoons vegetable oil

½ cup whole milk

½ cup sugar

1 large egg

1¼ cups all-purpose flour

2 teaspoons baking powder

½ teaspoon ground cinnamon

½ teaspoon nutmeg

pinch of salt

frying oil (peanut or canola oil recommended)

powdered sugar for garnish

*My guests always go crazy for these tender, bite-sized cake donuts. Instead of serving them in a bowl, I like to place three or four donuts in a small brown paper lunch bag and present them to each guest at the end of the meal. Then I wait for the surprise and joy on everyone's face when they open up their individual bag and inhale the intoxicating aroma of fresh donuts.*

In a mixing bowl with the paddle attachment, mix the first four ingredients on low speed until blended. Add the flour, baking powder, cinnamon, nutmeg, and salt. Mix until incorporated. Let batter rest while you warm the oil.

Add two inches of frying oil to a pot and heat it to 380°F. Using a spoon or ½-ounce scoop, drop about 1 tablespoon of batter into the oil and fry a few donuts at a time until golden brown, about 30 seconds per side. Transfer fried donuts to a wire rack. Repeat with remaining batter. Dust with powdered sugar before serving.

# CHEESE DANISH

MAKES 18 DANISH PASTRIES

**Dough:**

3½ cups all-purpose flour

1½ teaspoons salt

1 pound unsalted butter, cold and cubed

1 cup ice water

**Filling:**

8 ounces cream cheese, soft

¼ cup sugar

1 teaspoon pure almond extract

½ teaspoon pure vanilla extract

**Egg Wash:**

1 large egg

1 tablespoon water

*These buttery, flaky Danish pastries will blow your mind. The almond cream cheese center pairs extravagantly well with the light, crispy layers of pastry. Since this recipe yields many pastries, I usually freeze half the batch for future entertaining.*

In a mixing bowl with the paddle attachment, combine the flour and salt. Add the butter cubes and mix on low speed for 30 seconds. Increase speed to medium and mix until butter breaks down to pea size. Add the water all at once and mix just until dough comes together. Gather the dough into a disc and wrap with plastic. Let chill in refrigerator 20 minutes.

On a lightly floured surface, roll the dough out to a 12 × 30-inch rectangle. Fold the dough in thirds like a letter. Turn the dough 90° and repeat the roll and fold step, brushing any excess flour from the dough. Wrap in plastic and let chill in refrigerator 30 minutes.

Again, on a lightly floured surface, roll the dough out to a 12 × 30-inch rectangle. Fold the dough in thirds like a letter and chill for 30 minutes. Repeat this step one more time.

In a large bowl, stir together the cream cheese, sugar, and extracts until smooth. Set aside.

Line a sheet tray with parchment paper and set aside (line two sheet trays if making full batch). Remove dough from refrigerator and slice in half. Wrap one half and refrigerate, or freeze for later use. Roll the dough out into a ¼-inch-thick square and trim down to 12 × 12 inches with a pizza cutter. Cut out nine 4 × 4-inch squares, place on prepared tray, and keep cold in refrigerator. Repeat with other dough half, if using.

Whisk the egg and water in a small bowl. Brush the edges of each square with the egg wash. Add a tablespoon of cream cheese filling to the center of each square. Bring together opposite ends of the square up over filling and pinch tightly. You can leave as is or bring together the remaining opposite ends and again pinch to seal. After you finish shaping all the pastries, place them in the freezer for 20 minutes.

Preheat oven to 425°F. Brush with egg wash and bake for 20 minutes. Let cool for 5 minutes before serving.

# Nutella Pop Tarts

Makes 8 pastries

*Every time I eat one of these pop tarts, I find myself exclaiming, "These are so good!" The dough is super flaky and light. The Nutella, well, you know how good that stuff is. When paired together, this is an unforgettable combination.*

2 cups all-purpose flour

1 tablespoon sugar

1 teaspoon salt

1 cup unsalted butter, cold and cubed

1 cup ice water

1 large egg, separated

½ cup Nutella

powdered sugar for garnish

In a large mixing bowl with the paddle attachment, add the flour, sugar, and salt. Mix on low speed and slowly add the butter cubes. Increase speed to medium and continue until butter breaks down to pea size. Whisk together the water and egg yolk in a small bowl and add all at once to the mixer. Mix on low speed just until dough comes together. Form dough into two discs and wrap each in plastic. Let chill in refrigerator for 1 hour.

Line a sheet tray with parchment paper. Set aside another piece of parchment of the same size.

On a lightly floured surface, roll out one disc of dough into a 13 × 11-inch rectangle. Trim down to 12 × 10 inches with a sharp knife and then cut out eight 5 × 3-inch rectangles. Place on prepared sheet tray and cover with the extra parchment sheet. Repeat this step with the remaining disc of dough, place cutouts on the top parchment sheet, and then place sheet tray in refrigerator for about 20 minutes to chill the dough cutouts.

Slide off the top layer of parchment and its cutouts. These will be the tops of the pop tarts.

Poke some holes into the bottom cutouts with a fork. Whisk the egg white and, using a pastry brush, moisten their edges. Spread a tablespoon of Nutella down the center. Lay a top cutout over the filling and rub your fingertips around the edges to seal. Use the tines of the fork to double seal the edges and poke some holes on top. Place sheet tray in freezer for 1 hour.

Preheat oven to 375°F. Bake for 15 minutes. Cool completely. Garnish with sifted powdered sugar before serving.

# Savory Breads

Savory breads can serve as the foundation of a great brunch. Even guests who may be trying to limit their bread intake will inevitably break their self-imposed rules to sample the unique pull these breads create. Many of the following breads pair well with the recipes found in the Salads and Casseroles and Egg Dishes chapters.

The crispy Grissini breadsticks add a wonderful crunch to my Kale Salad, the Cinnamon Raisin Loaf is to die for, and many days I find myself enjoying my Blueberry Zucchini Bread for a breakfast on the go.

# GRISSINI

⅓ cup water

¼ cup whole milk

½ tablespoon active dry yeast

1 teaspoon sugar

1½ cups all-purpose flour

1 tablespoon olive oil

½ teaspoon salt

olive oil and salt

*Try serving these with my Kale Salad (see page 178).*

*Grissinis are crispy breadsticks that originated in Italy. I love having a jar of these on the table so guests can snack on something when they arrive. Grissinis also make great accompaniments to salads.*

Combine the water and milk and warm in the microwave. Stir in the yeast and sugar. Let sit for 5 minutes or until bubbles appear on the surface.

Add the flour, olive oil, and salt to a mixing bowl fitted with the dough attachment. Add the yeast mixture and mix for 3 minutes. Transfer dough (it will feel tight) to an oiled bowl, cover with a dish towel, and let rise in a warm place for 20 minutes.

Line two baking sheets with aluminum foil and brush some olive oil onto the foil. Transfer dough to a clean flat surface and shape into a 15-inch-long log. Cut into 20 equal pieces. Roll each piece to about 12 inches long. Place on the prepared baking sheets. Brush with olive oil and sprinkle with salt. Cover with a kitchen towel and let rise in a warm place for 10 minutes.

Preheat oven to 375°F. Bake for 10 minutes. Use tongs to flip over the breadsticks and bake until golden brown and crisp, about 16 minutes more. Remove from oven and brush with olive oil. Let cool completely before serving.

# LIGHT AND FLUFFY ROSEMARY ROLLS

MAKES 12 LARGE ROLLS

*Not everybody eats bread with their meal these days. That's why it's so important that any bread you serve be really good. These rolls have just the right amount of chewiness and an added touch of rosemary. Rest assured there will be no regrets at your table with these delicious rolls.*

In a small bowl, stir together the yeast, ½ cup of the warm water, and ½ teaspoon sugar. Let sit for 5 minutes for yeast to activate.

Add the remaining water, egg, butter, ¼ cup sugar, rosemary, and salt to a stand mixer fitted with the hook attachment. Add the yeast mixture to the bowl and mix on medium speed to incorporate ingredients. Add the flour all at once and mix on low speed for 30 seconds to bring dough together. Increase speed to medium and mix for another minute to develop gluten. Transfer dough to a large greased bowl. Cover with a dish towel and let rise in a warm place until doubled, about 1½ hours.

Grease a 13 × 9-inch pan and set aside. Punch down dough and transfer to a floured surface. Press dough down and shape into an 8½ × 11-inch rectangle. With a sharp knife, cut into 12 equal squares. Shape each square into a ball by cupping the dough and moving your hand against the counter in a counterclockwise direction (opposite if you're left-handed). Place in the prepared pan and repeat with the other pieces of dough. Cover pan with dish towel and let rise in a warm place for another hour or until rolls triple in size, about 1½ hours.

Preheat oven to 375°F. Bake rolls for 15 minutes. While rolls are baking, combine the rosemary and salt in a small bowl. Remove rolls from oven, brush tops with melted butter, and sprinkle with the rosemary salt.

*Dough:*

1 tablespoon instant dry yeast

1¼ cups warm water

½ teaspoon plus ¼ cup sugar

1 large egg

5 tablespoons unsalted butter, soft

1 tablespoon rosemary, finely chopped

1½ teaspoons salt

4 cups all-purpose flour

*Rosemary Salt:*

1 tablespoon rosemary, finely chopped

½ teaspoon sea salt

2 tablespoons unsalted butter, melted

# BLUEBERRY ZUCCHINI BREAD

MAKES ONE 9 × 5 × 3 LOAF

*I'm always surprised how enjoyable this bread is. The sweet blueberry flavor really shines through—so much so that guests often don't realize there's zucchini in it. This bread stays moist for days in an airtight container.*

Preheat oven to 350°F. Grease one 9 × 5 × 3-inch loaf pan and set aside.

Pile the blueberries and half the sugar on a large cutting board. Using a sharp knife, chop the blueberries into small pieces, working the sugar into the blueberries. Set aside.

In a large bowl, whisk the remaining sugar, eggs, and oil until incorporated. Stir in the grated zucchini and the blueberries. Add the flour, baking powder, baking soda, and cinnamon and mix until incorporated. Pour into prepared pan. Bake for 1 hour.

1 cup blueberries

1 cup sugar

2 large eggs

½ cup vegetable oil

1½ cups zucchini, grated

1½ cups all-purpose flour

1 teaspoon baking powder

1 teaspoon baking soda

1 teaspoon ground cinnamon

# TOASTED ENGLISH MUFFINS WITH ROASTED STRAWBERRY JAM

MAKES 12 MUFFINS

*Jam:*
1 pound strawberries, hulled and halved
¼ cup sugar
1 tablespoons balsamic vinegar
1 tablespoon Cointreau
⅛ teaspoon freshly ground pepper

*Muffins:*
14 ounces all-purpose flour
1¼ teaspoons instant dry yeast
1 teaspoon sugar
¼ teaspoon salt
1 tablespoon unsalted butter, cold
10 ounces water, lukewarm
6 tablespoons corn meal

*When cooking the muffins, don't be tempted to flip them over before 8 minutes. They really do need to be cooked that long on each side!*

*If you haven't yet made homemade English muffins, it's about time. They are incredibly easy to make and absolutely delicious. The accompanying strawberry jam is a great way to use up leftover strawberries and, not to mention, any extra jam makes an exceptional peanut butter and jelly sandwich.*

*Make jam:*
Preheat oven to 350°F. Toss all the ingredients together in a large bowl. Transfer to a 9-inch pie pan and roast in the oven for 45 to 50 minutes, stirring occasionally, until juice thickens. Remove from oven and break up the fruit with a large spoon or a potato masher. Let cool completely on the counter. Juice will thicken as it cools. Transfer to an air-tight container and store in refrigerator.

*Make muffins:*
In a mixer fitted with the paddle attachment, combine the flour, yeast, sugar, salt, and butter. Mix on low speed to break up the butter. Add all the water and mix for 1 minute on low speed. Transfer dough to a greased bowl, cover with a dish towel, and let rise 30 minutes in a warm place. Meanwhile, line a sheet tray with parchment or aluminum foil, grease with cooking spray, and sprinkle 4 tablespoons of the corn meal on top. Set aside.

Punch dough down and transfer to a floured surface. Roll the dough to ½-inch thickness. Using a 3-inch round cutter, punch out muffins. Re-roll scraps as necessary. Place muffins on the prepared sheet tray. Sprinkle remaining corn meal on tops of dough. Cover with a dish towel and let rise for 30 minutes in a warm place.

When doubled in size, the muffins are ready to be cooked. Warm a large nonstick skillet over low to medium heat, grease with cooking spray, and cook muffins 8 minutes on each side until lightly browned.

# WHITE BREAD

*Growing up in Pennsylvania, I used to go to a small Amish-run restaurant in a nearby town. I'd always order their potato soup with white bread. While the soup was delicious, what I remember most was the white bread. It had a slightly sweet flavor, soft crumb, and firm texture. This is my best attempt at replicating that amazing bread.*

2 cups warm water

½ cup sugar

1 tablespoon active dry yeast

¼ cup unsalted butter, melted

1½ teaspoons salt

6 cups all-purpose flour

1 egg white

Whisk the water, ¼ cup sugar, and yeast in a small bowl and let sit for 5 minutes to activate yeast.

Add the butter, remaining sugar, and salt to a mixing bowl and stir to combine. Add the flour, followed by the yeast mixture, and mix on low speed with the hook attachment for 2 minutes. Transfer the dough to an oiled stainless steel bowl, cover with a dish towel, and let rise in a warm place until doubled, about 1 hour.

Grease two 9 x 5 x 3 loaf pans and set aside. Punch down dough and divide into two equal pieces. Roll each into the shape of a log and place into the prepared loaf pans. Cover with a dish towel and let rise in a warm place until dough rises just above the top of the pans, about 30 minutes. Preheat oven to 350°F.

Whisk the egg white well and brush over each loaf. Bake for 30 minutes. Let cool completely on counter before slicing.

# MULTIGRAIN BOULE

## MAKES 1 BOULE

*This nutritious, no-knead bread could not be any easier to make. The dough comes together quickly with minimal effort. After rising overnight, the dough is loosely shaped and baked in a piping hot oven. In less than an hour, you'll have delicious homemade bread all your guests will surely savor. I recommend using a Dutch oven to guarantee a crispy crust and soft interior, but any sturdy oven-proof pot with lid will work.*

2 cups all-purpose flour

2 cups whole wheat flour

¼ cup raw sunflower seeds

¼ cup flaxseeds

2 teaspoons salt

1 teaspoon sugar

¾ teaspoon instant yeast

2 cups water, lukewarm

½ cup rolled oats

*The night before:*
Combine the flours, seeds, salt, sugar, and yeast in a large stainless steel bowl. Add all the water and stir with a rubber spatula until dough forms. Shape into a loose ball (it doesn't have to be perfect), cover bowl with a dish towel, and let sit on the counter for 12 hours.

*The next morning:*
Place a 5-quart Dutch oven with lid onto the center rack and turn oven on to 450°F.

Transfer the dough onto a floured counter and shape into a ball. Sprinkle some oats onto the counter and place the ball of dough onto the oats to coat its bottom. Then pat the remaining oats onto the top of the dough. Drop the dough into the warmed pot and bake covered for 30 minutes. Remove lid and bake another 20 minutes. Let cool completely before slicing.

# Sunflower and Flaxseed Bagels

MAKES 8 BAGELS

*Every time I make these bagels, I end up eating two straight out of the oven. They're squishy with a crisp bite and chewy interior, just like a great bagel should be.*

❖❖❖❖❖❖❖❖❖❖❖❖❖❖❖❖❖❖❖❖❖❖❖❖❖❖❖❖❖❖❖❖❖❖❖❖❖❖❖❖❖❖❖❖❖❖❖❖❖❖❖❖❖❖❖❖❖❖❖❖

*Make bagels:*
Mix ½ cup of the warm water, sugar, and yeast in a small bowl. Let sit for 5 minutes to activate yeast.

Add the flour and salt to a mixing bowl with the hook attachment. Add the yeast mixture along with the remaining cup of warm water. Mix on low speed for 4 minutes to develop gluten. Transfer dough to an oiled bowl, cover with dish towel, and let rise for 30 minutes in a warm place.

Line a sheet tray with aluminum foil and coat with cooking spray. Punch dough down and transfer to a lightly floured surface. Cut into 8 equal pieces and shape each into a ball. Press your floured thumb into the center of one of the dough balls and poke your fingers through from underneath, stretching the hole to about two inches wide. Place on the prepared sheet tray and repeat with the remaining dough balls. Cover them with a dish towel and let rise in a warm place for 10 minutes while you prepare the water boil.

*Make water boil:*
Bring 3 quarts water to a rolling boil in a large pot over high heat. Stir in the malt syrup and baking soda and reduce to a gentle boil. Drop in 3 bagels at a time, cooking them 1 minute on each side. Transfer to a dish towel with a slotted spoon. Repeat with the remaining bagels. Discard water. Preheat oven to 425°F.

Re-line the sheet tray with new aluminum foil and coat with cooking spray. Mix the sunflower and flaxseeds in a medium bowl. Brush the tops of the boiled bagels with the whisked egg. Firmly press the tops of them into the seeds and place on the sheet tray.

Bake for 15 minutes, rotate, then 10 minutes more.

*Bagels:*

1½ cups warm water

1 tablespoon sugar

2 teaspoons active dry yeast

4 cups all-purpose flour

2 teaspoons salt

*Water Boil:*

3 quarts water

1 tablespoon barley malt syrup

1 tablespoon baking soda

*Garnish:*

½ cup raw hulled sunflower seeds

½ cup flaxseeds

1 egg, whisked

*You can find barley malt syrup at natural food stores, typically near the peanut butter section.*

# PINEAPPLE CHALLAH

MAKES 1 BRAIDED LOAF

1 cup water, lukewarm

1 tablespoon instant yeast

⅓ cup sugar

2 large eggs

1 large egg yolk

4½ cups all-purpose flour

4 tablespoons unsalted butter, melted

4 tablespoons canola oil

2 teaspoons salt

6 ounces dried pineapple, chopped into small bits

1 large egg for glazing

*Though it may look complicated, challah is actually one of the easier breads to make. The bits of dried pineapple in my version add a subtle hint of sweetness. You can use this challah to make delectable French toast, as well.*

Place the water, yeast, and sugar in a mixing bowl and stir to dissolve. Add the eggs, yolk, flour, butter, oil, and salt and mix for 1 minute on low speed with the hook attachment. Increase to medium speed for 30 seconds. Transfer dough to an oiled bowl, cover with dish towel, and let rise in a warm place for 1½ hours.

Line a sheet tray with greased aluminum foil and set aside. Transfer dough to a clean, flat surface and cut into two equal pieces. Roll each one out to a 24-inch-long strand. Then use a rolling pin to flatten them out to about 3 inches wide. Spread the pineapple bits down the center of the strips. Roll each one up lengthwise like a roulade. Pinch the ends to seal.

Form one strand into a boomerang shape and lay it flat on the counter. Shape the other strand similarly and place its left half on top of the first boomerang such that its arms become the second and fourth strands. Fold the first strand over the second. Fold the fourth strand under the third and over the second. Make sure your folds are snug. Repeat folds until braid is formed. Tuck the ends under the loaf and transfer to the prepared sheet tray. Cover with dish towel and let rise for 1 hour in a warm place.

Preheat oven to 350°F. Whisk the egg and brush it onto the loaf. Bake for 40 minutes until golden brown or until loaf sounds hollow when tapped.

# Cinnamon Raisin Loaf

MAKES ONE 9 × 5 × 3 LOAF

*Dough:*

¼ cup sherry

1 cup dark raisins

⅓ cup warm water

1 teaspoon instant dry yeast

½ teaspoon sugar

½ cup whole milk

1 large egg

1 tablespoon sugar

¼ teaspoon salt

5 tablespoons unsalted butter, melted

2½ cups all-purpose flour

*Filling:*

½ cup sugar

1 teaspoon ground cinnamon

*Place a loaf of this bread on the table and I guarantee you'll be greeted by oohs and aahs all around. It's heavenly as-is or toasted with butter. Though this recipe makes one loaf, you may as well go ahead and double it—it's that good!*

In a small saucepan, bring the sherry to a boil over high heat. Stir in the raisins and cook for 1 minute or until most of the sherry evaporates. Set aside to cool.

In a small bowl, stir together the warm water, yeast, and sugar. Let sit for 5 minutes to activate yeast.

Combine the milk, egg, sugar, salt, 1 tablespoon of melted butter, and the raisins in a mixing bowl fitted with the hook attachment. Mix on low speed to combine ingredients. Add the yeast, followed by the flour. Mix on low speed until dough forms. Continue to mix for another 30 seconds to knead dough and develop gluten. Transfer dough to a greased bowl, cover with a dish towel, and place in a warm area until doubled in size.

Combine the sugar and cinnamon in a small bowl and set aside. Grease a 9 × 5 × 3-inch loaf pan and set aside.

After dough rises, punch down dough and transfer to a lightly floured surface. Roll out to a 16 × 8-inch rectangle. Brush the surface with the melted butter, leaving about a tablespoon for later. Sprinkle the cinnamon-sugar mixture over the butter, leaving about a tablespoon for later. Tightly roll up the dough, starting from one of the shorter sides. Transfer the dough to the prepared loaf pan, seam-side down. Cover with a dish towel and let rise in a warm area until doubled in size, about 45 minutes. Dough will rise above the top edge of the pan.

Preheat oven to 400°F. Brush top of loaf with half of the remaining melted butter and sprinkle with half of the remaining cinnamon sugar. Bake for 20 minutes. Reduce heat to 375°F and bake for an additional 15 minutes. Remove from oven, brush with remaining butter, and top with remaining cinnamon sugar. Let cool completely before slicing.

*Beach House Porridge*

# Grains

In my world of food, when it grains, it pours. What I mean is: every few months I get on a grain kick and it lasts for a couple weeks. Then it's back to the dry spell. No doubt grains, especially whole grains, are good for you; we all need to be eating more of them. My theory is to make something wonderful available in this category, and someone at the table will be bold enough to be the first to try it. It may even compel others to bring grains back into their food lives. Here are some delicious recipes that will help you win some converts.

**Beach House Porridge**

**90**

**Maple and Date Steel-Cut Oatmeal with Orange Mascarpone**

**91**

**Quinoa and Chard Breakfast Bowl**

**93**

**Shrimp N' Grits**

**94**

**Beach's Best Granola II**

**97**

**Sooji**

**99**

# BEACH HOUSE PORRIDGE

MAKES 4 SERVINGS

*Porridge:*

½ cup rolled oats

½ cup long grain rice

¼ cup pearl barley

¼ cup farina

5½ cups water

1 cup whole milk

1-inch vanilla bean, split

1-inch cinnamon stick

*Garnishes:*

½ cup dark raisins +
    1 cup water

½ cup whole pecans

1 (6-ounce) package
    blueberries + 1½
    tablespoons sugar +
    1 tablespoon water

*This comforting porridge is thick and creamy and showcases a slew of differing textures thanks to the oats, rice, pearl barley, and farina. It's a nice change from popular cereal dishes like oatmeal and Cream of Wheat.*

*Make porridge:*
In a medium pot, combine the oats, rice, pearl barley, and farina and stir to combine. Add the water, milk, vanilla bean, and cinnamon stick. Place over medium heat and bring mixture to a low simmer. Cook for 40 minutes, stirring occasionally.

*While porridge cooks, prepare garnishes:*
Bring the raisins and 1 cup of water to a boil in a small pot over high heat. Cover, remove from heat, and let sit 10 minutes. Strain and set raisins aside.

In a small sauté pan over high heat, toast the pecans until fragrant and lightly browned, shaking frequently, about 5 minutes. Set aside.

Combine the blueberries, sugar, and water in a small pot and bring to a boil for 3 minutes until thickened. Break a few berries to release their juices. Set aside.

When porridge is fully cooked, portion out into four bowls and garnish with the plumped raisins, toasted pecans, and blueberries.

*If you want a creamier porridge, substitute with short grain rice.*

# Maple and Date Steel-Cut Oatmeal with Orange Mascarpone

Makes 4 servings

*When steel-cut oats are cooked, they morph into porridge with a hearty texture and nutty taste. Cooking them with dates, an all-natural sweetener, keeps this dish heart-healthy while the orange mascarpone adds bright notes and decadence.*

6 cups water

2 cups steel-cut oats

16 pitted dates, brunoised, plus more for garnish

⅛ teaspoon salt

1 (5-ounce) package mascarpone fresca

1 teaspoon orange zest

2 tablespoons pure maple syrup, plus more for garnish

In a large pot, bring the water to a boil over high heat. Add the oats, chopped dates, and salt. Reduce heat to medium and continue cooking for 20 minutes, stirring occasionally. The oatmeal will thicken as it cooks.

Meanwhile, in a small bowl, stir together the mascarpone and orange zest. Keep in refrigerator.

Remove the oats from heat and stir in the maple syrup. Serve warm with additional maple syrup, chopped dates, and the orange mascarpone.

# QUINOA AND CHARD BREAKFAST BOWL

MAKES 2 SERVINGS

*This tasty vegetarian breakfast bowl is filling, high in fiber, and packed with antioxidants.*

Cook the 2 eggs to soft boil stage as directed on page 105. Set aside.

Place quinoa, water, and salt in a small pot. Bring to a boil, reduce to a simmer, cover, and cook for 15 minutes. Set aside.

Melt the butter and oil in a large sauté pan over medium heat. Add the onions and garlic and cook for 2 minutes. Add the chard, salt, and pepper, and cook until leaves are wilted, about 3 minutes. Add the quinoa and stir until incorporated.

Divide the quinoa mixture between two serving bowls. Top with avocado slices and microgreens. Place the soft-boiled eggs on the rivets of a cutting board. Smash eggs with a fork, carefully transfer to the bowls, and top with a dash of salt and pepper.

2 large eggs

1 cup quinoa

2 cups water

¼ teaspoon salt

1 tablespoon unsalted butter

1 tablespoon olive oil

¼ cup thinly sliced red onion

3 cloves garlic, minced

1 bunch red Swiss chard, stems trimmed, leaves chiffonade

¼ teaspoon salt

¼ teaspoon pepper

1 ripe avocado

1 package microgreen sprouts

salt and pepper

# SHRIMP N' GRITS

MAKES 4 SERVINGS

1 pound large shrimp, deveined and peeled
1 tablespoon Cajun seasoning
2 cups water
1 cup chicken broth
2 tablespoons unsalted butter
1 cup quick-cook grits
4 ounces white cheddar, shredded
2 ounces American grana, shredded
¼ teaspoon salt
¼ teaspoon ground pepper
3 strips bacon, cut into bits
3 ounces shiitake mushrooms, thinly sliced
2 scallions, chopped
1 clove garlic, minced
1 lemon, halved
¼ cup all-purpose flour
½ cup chicken broth
¼ teaspoon tabasco sauce
¼ cup chopped parsley
1 tablespoon unsalted butter
salt and pepper to taste

*This Southern low country dish is deeply satisfying. It combines the smoothness of cheese grits with the slight snap of shrimp and a tinge of tabasco. Don't be fooled by the long list of ingredients; the dish actually comes together pretty fast.*

Toss the shrimp with the Cajun seasoning in a medium bowl and set aside.

Bring the water, broth, and butter to a boil in a medium pot over high heat. Add the grits and cook over medium heat for 3 minutes, whisking occasionally. Remove from heat and whisk in the cheeses, salt, and pepper. Cover and set aside.

In a large sauté pan over high heat, cook the bacon bits for 3 minutes, stirring occasionally. Add the mushrooms and cook for 3 minutes more. Season with salt and pepper. Add the scallions, garlic, and the juice of a lemon half. Cook 2 minutes. Stir in the flour. Add the broth and tabasco and scrape the pan bottom with a rubber spatula to dissolve the bits. Let mixture gently boil for 1 minute. Add the shrimp and cook for 2 minutes. Stir in parsley and butter. Let mixture cook 1 minute more. Season with salt and pepper.

Transfer grits to four dishes. Top the grits with the shrimp mixture. Cut the remaining lemon half into four wedges and use as a garnish on each plate.

# Beach's Best Granola II

Makes 4 cups

*For those of you who are familiar with my first cookbook, you may recognize the name of this recipe. This is a new and choice version of the granola recipe I shared in* Beach House Baking. *I hope you enjoy it!*

3 cups rolled oats

½ cup pecans, roughly chopped

½ cup pepitas

1 teaspoon ground cinnamon

⅓ cup olive oil

⅓ cup orange blossom honey

1 teaspoon pure vanilla extract

1 cup dried cranberries

Preheat oven to 300°F. Line two sheet trays with aluminum foil and set aside.

Combine the oats, pecans, pepitas, and cinnamon in a large bowl.

In a small pot, boil the oil, honey, and vanilla over high heat. Pour over the oat mixture and stir together well with a rubber spatula until oats are evenly coated. Divide mixture evenly between the two prepared sheet trays.

Bake for 15 minutes. Stir granola and bake for another 15 minutes. Let cool completely before tossing with the cranberries. Store in an airtight container.

# Sooji

*Sooji is a sweet breakfast cereal popular in India that's made with farina. My mom taught me this recipe when I was very little, and it has remained one of my favorite breakfast dishes ever since.*

Stir together the water, sugar, and cardamom in a small pot. Place over high heat. When mixture begins to boil, remove from heat and set aside.

Place the farina in a large sauté pan over medium heat. Cook the farina until lightly browned and fragrant, about 8 minutes. Stir or shake frequently to ensure even cooking. Be aware that the mixture may smoke slightly during last couple minutes of cooking. Transfer browned farina to a plate.

Add butter to the pan and return to heat. Add the raisins and cook them in the butter for 1 minute. Raisins will puff up and butter will brown. Add the farina all at once and stir to combine. Mixture will resemble sand. Remove from heat.

Carefully remove and discard the cardamom pods from the sugar water and slowly pour a cup of it to the farina in the pan. Splashing may occur, so use a rubber spatula with a long handle to stir in the water. Return to low heat and continue stirring until the water is absorbed, a few seconds. Add the remaining water in three more portions, stirring after each addition. After the last addition, continue stirring for about 30 more seconds to dry the mixture to your desired consistency. Transfer Sooji to bowls and serve warm.

2½ cups water

⅓ cup sugar

5 cardamom pods, open

1 cup farina

5 tablespoons unsalted butter, soft

¼ cup dark raisins

*Some of you may find this Sooji recipe too sweet for your taste buds. Feel free to adjust the amount of sugar accordingly.*

# Egg Dishes

Egg dishes are the pièce de résistance of brunch menus everywhere. My guests always look forward to seeing which egg dishes make the centerpiece of my brunches. In this largest chapter of the book, I've showcased how to feature eggs in new and interesting ways as well as traditionally with a little more edge. Some of my favorites include Eggs Milanese, Stuffed Quiche, and Eggs Wellington. So don't wait a minute more—crack open this chapter and get cooking.

# HOW TO FRY AN EGG

1 tablespoon unsalted butter, soft

1 large egg, room temperature

salt and pepper

*Yes, I know many of you already know how to fry an egg and likely see no reason to change your proven method. If that's the case, then by all means, turn the page—no hard feelings, sort of. However, for many of you (including myself), something so basic can often cause much stress. Throughout the writing of this book, I tested various ways of frying an egg: butter versus oil, high versus low heat, covered versus uncovered. In the end, the winning method was: cook covered with butter over low heat. Follow this mantra, and each time you will be blessed with a scrumptious fried egg with a soft but firm white and a gorgeous, runny yolk.*

In a heavy-bottomed sauté pan, melt the butter over medium heat until melted, not foamy. Crack the egg into the center, reduce heat to low, and cover. Leave undisturbed for 3 minutes. Remove from heat, season with salt and pepper, and serve immediately.

# BOILED EGGS

*Boiled eggs are delicious and I love the versatility of this cooking method. However, the title of this recipe is slightly misleading as you actually don't want to cook the eggs in boiling water per se. Boiling them causes the eggs to dry out quickly, discolor, and lose their wonderful flavor. After much testing during the writing of this book, I came up with a handy chart for how best to achieve delicious "boiled eggs" of varying stages.*

The cooking times below are based on four eggs, straight from the refrigerator. Before cooking them, use the pointy end of a pestle to make a slight crack at the rounded bottom of the eggs. This will make them easier to peel afterward. Be careful—you don't want to break the membrane, just release some of the pressure. Place the eggs in a heavy-bottomed pot that comfortably fits them with room to move. You want the water to completely surround the eggs to ensure even cooking. Fill the pot with warm water to about an inch above the eggs and place over high heat. As soon as the water reaches a boil—the moment the first energetic bubble breaks the surface—remove from heat, cover, and let sit according to the chart below.

| COOKING TIME (minutes) | STAGE | DESCRIPTION | USES |
|---|---|---|---|
| 2 | Soft Runny | Runny white, raw yolk | Egg cup |
| 3 | Soft | Set white, runny yolk | Over hashes, breakfast bowls |
| 5 | Soft Medium | Set white, tender yolk with wet center | Salads |
| 8 | Medium Hard | Solid white, set yolk but moist | Alone, in sandwiches |
| 10 | Hard | Solid white, solid yolk | Deviled eggs |

Strain eggs into a colander and rinse with cold water for 10 seconds. Let eggs rest for a couple minutes. Crack the shell all over. Starting from the rounded bottom end where the air pocket is, carefully peel off the shell.

*Did you know you can use a martini shaker to peel hard-boiled eggs? Place two hard-boiled eggs in the shaker and fill with cold water until eggs are submerged. Shake vigorously for a few seconds. Remove eggs and you'll discover that the shells slide off easily.*

# DEVILED EGGS

## MAKES 12 PORTIONS

6 large eggs

¼ cup mayonnaise

¼ cup minced celery

1 teaspoon chives, chopped

1 teaspoon horseradish sauce

1 teaspoon sweet relish

¼ teaspoon tabasco sauce

⅛ teaspoon salt

⅛ teaspoon pepper

paprika and chives, for garnish

*I don't eat deviled eggs often, but when I do, it's a problem. I always forget how appetizing they are and somehow end up eating far too many of these snack-sized treats. They're a great way to incorporate an egg dish into your brunch when you're short on time.*

Cook eggs to hard-boiled stage as directed on page 105. Peels shells, dry eggs well with paper towels, and slice in half lengthwise with a sharp knife.

Remove yolks (I find it easiest to pull the white away from the yolk with your hands) and place them into a medium stainless steel bowl. Break up the clumps of yolk with a whisk. Add the remaining ingredients and mix well with a rubber spatula. Use a baby spoon to fill the egg whites. Sprinkle with paprika and top with chives. If not serving immediately, place in an airtight container in refrigerator.

# PERFECT POACHED EGGS

6 cups water

1 teaspoon white vinegar

1 teaspoon salt

6 large eggs

salt and pepper

*Poached eggs are my favorite way to prepare eggs. The light, fluffy whites and warm, creamy yolks are delectable. Vinegar in this recipe helps the whites set faster and straining the whites before poaching limits the wispy bits. You'll need a small mesh strainer and a slotted spatula for this one.*

Bring water, vinegar, and salt to a boil in a 3-quart (2-inch deep) saucepan over high heat. Decrease heat and bring to a very low simmer. Set a small mesh strainer over a cup and crack an egg into the strainer. Let sit for a few seconds to strain the loose egg whites. Carefully slide the egg into the water at the 12 o'clock position. Strain the remaining eggs one at a time and add to the pot at the 5 o'clock, 7, 2, 10, and center position. Cover with lid and set timer for 3 minutes.

Using a slotted spatula, carefully remove the eggs, starting with the one you added first, and transfer to a paper towel. Season with salt and pepper. Serve immediately.

# Italian Meats Quiche

MAKES ONE 9½-INCH QUICHE

*This quiche is quick to pull together, making it the perfect recipe for a last-minute brunch. It packs a lot of flavor thanks to the savory spread of cured Italian meats. Sautéing the meats beforehand releases fat and enhances flavor. For any of your guests who are worried about quiche not being robust enough for their appetite or self-image, this quiche answers all questions.*

**Crust:**

1¼ cups all-purpose flour

½ teaspoon salt

½ teaspoon sugar

4 ounces unsalted butter, cold and cubed

3 tablespoons ice water

**Filling:**

1 ounce <u>each</u> mortadella, prosciutto, Genoa salami, and capocolla

¼ cup minced red onion

3 ounces (about 5 slices) provolone

**Custard:**

4 large eggs

2 cups half-and-half

¼ teaspoon salt

⅛ teaspoon ground pepper

⅛ teaspoon ground nutmeg

*Make crust:*
Combine the flour, salt, and sugar in a stand mixer with the paddle attachment. Add the cubed butter and mix on medium speed until pea size. Add the water and mix just until dough starts coming together. Gather into a ball with your hands, transfer to a floured surface, and form into a disc. Roll out to a 12-inch round and line a 10-inch pie tin. Trim and flute the edges, prick holes in the dough with a fork, and place in refrigerator to chill. (Note: If it's a warm day, chill the dough for 10 minutes in the refrigerator before rolling out.)

*Make filling:*
Working with a few meat slices at a time, roll them up and cut into ¼-inch slices. After all the meat has been sliced, sauté them together in a large pan over medium high heat until slightly crisped and browned, about 3 minutes. Remove meats and let drain on a paper towel. Add the minced onion to the pan and sauté for 2 minutes. Set aside.

Preheat oven to 350°F. Place a sheet tray on center rack. You will bake the quiche on this tray.

Just as you did with the meats, roll up the provolone and cut into ¼-inch slices. Set aside.

*Make custard:*
In a large bowl, whisk the eggs, half-and-half, salt, pepper, and nutmeg. Stir in the sautéed onions and sliced provolone. Arrange the meats in the pie shell. Slowly pour the egg mixtures over the meats. Place quiche on the sheet tray and bake for 40 minutes or until an inserted knife comes out clean.

# HUMBLE EGG SANDWICH

### Greens:
1 tablespoon lemon juice

1 tablespoon balsamic vinegar

1 teaspoon Dijon mustard

¼ cup olive oil

salt and pepper, to taste

2 cups baby arugula

### Sandwich:
12 slices bacon, each strip cut in half

1 loaf of White Bread (see page 79 for recipe)

½ cup mayonnaise

4 tablespoons unsalted butter, soft

4 large eggs

4 (¼-inch) rings of red onion

*There's nothing fancy about the ingredients in this recipe, but somehow a runny fried egg, peppery arugula, salty bacon, and sweet red onion combine to make this scrumptious breakfast sandwich. You can use a store-bought hard roll, but I highly recommend using my White Bread (page 79).*

*Make greens:*

In a medium bowl, combine the lemon juice, vinegar, and mustard. Whisk in the oil and season with salt and pepper. Toss 2 tablespoons of the vinaigrette with the arugula in a small bowl and set aside. Store the remaining vinaigrette in the refrigerator for future use.

*Make sandwich:*

Preheat oven to 400°F. Line a baking sheet with aluminum foil. Snugly weave 6 strips of bacon, 3 in each direction, on the foil. Repeat with remaining bacon strips. Bake for 20 minutes. Flip lattices over with tongs and bake 5 minutes more. Transfer bacon lattices to a paper towel to drain.

Using a serrated knife, cut the White Bread into 8 slices. Toast them and spread mayonnaise on each slice. Top four of them with the bacon lattices.

Melt the butter in a large sauté pan over medium heat. Add the eggs, leaving space between. Turn heat to low. Cover and cook for 3 minutes until whites are firm and tops are set. Lay an egg onto each bacon lattice. Top each egg with an onion ring and some arugula. Sandwich with the remaining toasts.

# BAKED EGGS MILANESE

### Baked eggs:

2 tablespoons olive oil

3 cloves garlic, thinly sliced

2 red vine tomatoes, sliced ¼-inch thick

10 large eggs

¼ teaspoon salt

⅛ teaspoon pepper

### Broiled asparagus:

1 bunch asparagus

2 tablespoons olive oil

⅛ teaspoon salt

⅛ teaspoon pepper

small block of parmesan for shaving

*This is my version of the popular asparagus and egg dish seen in Italy. Baking the eggs allows the flavors of tomato and garlic to absorb and results in delicious soft, fluffy eggs.*

Preheat oven to 375°F.

Heat the olive oil in a large sauté pan over medium heat. Add the garlic slices and stir for one minute. Add the tomato slices to the pan, covering the bottom of the pan completely. Cook for 1 minute, then flip tomatoes over and cook for an additional minute.

Whisk the eggs, salt, and pepper in a large bowl and slowly add to the pan, gently enough so the tomatoes don't float to the top. Cover pan and place in oven. Bake for 15 minutes.

While eggs bake, trim away the asparagus bottoms and toss the stalks with olive oil, salt, and pepper in a large bowl. Transfer to a brownie pan.

When eggs are done baking, remove from oven and set aside (keep the lid on). Adjust oven to broil and cook asparagus for 5 minutes. Shake pan and broil for another 5 minutes. Time may vary depending on thickness of asparagus.

Invert eggs onto a serving plate. Top with the broiled asparagus and parmesan shavings. Serve immediately.

# CHIVE AND CHEDDAR OMELET

*It's easy to get carried away by adding too many ingredients when making an omelet. When this happens, the wonderful flavor of egg gets lost. In this simple and delicious omelet, the sharp cheddar and chive complement the soft egg and showcase what an omelet is really is all about.*

½ tablespoon unsalted butter, soft

1 tablespoon chives, chopped

2 large eggs

pinch of salt and pepper

¼ cup sharp cheddar, shredded

Warm an 8-inch sauté pan over medium heat. Melt the butter in the pan. Stir in half of the chives and cook for 15 seconds.

Vigorously whisk the eggs, remaining chives, salt, and pepper in a small bowl and pour into the pan. Reduce heat to low. Let eggs cook underlined for 3 minutes. Use a rubber spatula to gently move any uncooked eggs on top toward the edges, where the eggs cook faster. Continue slow cooking the eggs until they're nearly dry (you want some uncooked egg left on top since it will continue cooking after you fold the omelet). Sprinkle the cheese down the center of the omelet. Gently flip a third of the egg over the cheese and then roll out onto a plate. Serve immediately.

# Roasted Red Pepper, Goat Cheese, and Caramelized Onion Tart

*I love making tarts for brunches. They're easy to make and can feed many mouths. Guests will love this tart's trio of smoky red peppers, tangy goat cheese, and sweet onions.*

**Crust:**

1½ cups all-purpose flour

¼ teaspoon salt

4½ ounces unsalted butter, cold and cubed

4 tablespoons ice water

**Filling:**

2 medium red bell peppers

1 tablespoon olive oil

salt for sprinkling

2 tablespoons unsalted butter

1 large yellow onion, peeled, halved, and thinly sliced

2 tablespoons sugar

1 teaspoon salt

4 ounces goat cheese

**Custard:**

1 large egg

½ cup half-and-half

¼ teaspoon salt

⅛ teaspoon pepper

*Make crust:*

In a mixing bowl with the paddle attachment, mix the flour and salt. Add the cubed butter and mix on low speed until mixture resembles coarse crumbs. Add the water and mix just until dough starts to come together. Shape into a disc, wrap with plastic, and let chill in refrigerator one hour.

*Make filling:*

Turn broiler on high. In a large bowl, coat the peppers with the olive oil and lightly sprinkle with salt. Transfer peppers onto a foil-lined sheet tray and place under the broiler, turning them every 4 to 5 minutes until evenly charred on all sides. Transfer peppers to a plate and let cool.

In a large sauté pan over high heat, melt the butter and add the onions, sugar, and salt. Stir occasionally and continue to cook until the onions caramelize, about 12 to 15 minutes. Remove from heat and set aside to cool. Meanwhile, julienne or small dice the roasted peppers, discarding the stem and seeds.

Preheat oven to 375°F. Remove dough from refrigerator and roll out the dough between two pieces of parchment or wax paper to a 12-inch circle. Remove top paper and flip dough over onto your tart pan. Press dough into the pan and trim edges to a ½-inch overhang. Fold inward and press evenly into the sides of the tart pan. Prick holes in the dough with a fork. Line with parchment or aluminum foil, fill with pie weights (rice or beans work well, too), and bake 15 minutes.

*Continued on page 117*

Crumble half the goat cheese into the par-baked tart shell, followed by half the red peppers and half the onions. Repeat.

*Make custard:*
In a small bowl, whisk together the egg, half-and-half, salt, and pepper. Slowly pour over the filling. Bake until the custard is set, about 15 to 20 minutes. Let rest for at least 10 minutes before slicing.

# LEEK TART

### Crust:
- 1½ cups all-purpose flour
- ¼ teaspoon salt
- 4½ ounces unsalted butter, cold and cubed
- 4 tablespoons ice water

### Leek Filling:
- 5–6 large leeks (to yield 1 pound after trimming)
- 2 tablespoons unsalted butter, soft
- ½ teaspoon salt
- ⅛ teaspoon pepper

### Custard:
- 2 large eggs
- 1 cup half-and-half
- 2 teaspoons Dijon mustard
- ½ teaspoon salt
- ¼ teaspoon pepper
- ⅛ teaspoon nutmeg

*Popular in Northern France, the leek tart doesn't get enough credit. Many people think leeks are only good for potato soup, but they actually make a delectable tart. My secret ingredient is a little Dijon mustard to help improve flavor and make this tart unforgettable.*

*Make crust:*

In a stand mixer with the paddle attachment, mix the flour and salt. Add the cubed butter and mix on low speed until mixture resembles coarse crumbs. Add the water and mix just until dough starts to come together. Shape into a disc, wrap with plastic, and let chill in refrigerator 1 hour.

*Make leek filling:*

Trim leeks, leaving only the white and tender green parts. Split lengthwise and cut into ¼-inch slices. Place in colander and rinse well to remove dirt. Dry well with paper towels.

In a large sauté pan, melt butter over medium heat. Stir in the leeks, salt and, pepper. Cover and stir occasionally until pale and very soft, about 25 minutes. Remove from heat.

Preheat oven to 375°F. Place sheet tray on middle rack. Remove dough from refrigerator and roll out the dough between two pieces of parchment or wax paper to a 12-inch circle. Remove top paper and flip over onto your tart pan. Press dough into the pan and trim edges to a ½-inch overhang. Fold inward and press evenly into the sides of the tart pan. Prick holes in the dough with a fork. Line with parchment or aluminum foil, fill with pie weights (rice or beans work fine, too), and bake 15 minutes.

*Make custard:*

While shell is baking, whisk the eggs, half-and-half, mustard, salt, pepper, and nutmeg in a large bowl. Stir in the cooked leeks and then pour mixture into the par-baked tart shell. Use a fork to evenly distribute the leeks if needed. Bake until the custard is set, about 15 to 20 minutes. Let rest for at least 10 minutes before slicing.

# CLAY POT STEAMED EGGS (*GYERAN JJIM*)

MAKES 2 SERVINGS

*I first had this dish during a dinner out for Korean barbeque. Though it's commonly served as a side dish, I find it equally satisfying as a morning meal. Clay pots are available at Chinese grocery stores and online cookware sites. Make sure to follow the manufacturer instructions for the preparation and care of your clay pot before and after use.*

1 cup chicken broth

1 scallion, chopped

1 clove garlic, minced

¼ teaspoon red chili flakes

3 large eggs, whisked

¼ teaspoon salt

¼ teaspoon ground pepper

white rice for serving

Combine the chicken broth, half of the chopped scallions, garlic, and chili flakes in a medium clay pot. Bring to a rolling boil over medium heat. Reduce heat to low.

Whisk the eggs, salt, and pepper in a small bowl and stir them into the broth for a few seconds. Cover and cook for 4 to 5 minutes until eggs resemble soft tofu. Remove from heat, top with remaining scallions, and serve immediately with warm white rice.

*Be careful, clay pots get very hot. Make sure to place on a heat-proof mat when serving.*

# BREAKFAST TACOS

MAKES 6 TACOS

*Pico de Gallo:*

2 vine tomatoes, small diced

½ cup thinly sliced red onion

¼ cup cilantro, chopped

1 serrano chili, thinly sliced

⅛ teaspoon salt

⅛ teaspoon pepper

Juice of one lime

*Tacos:*

6 small flour tortillas

4 tablespoons unsalted butter

6 large eggs

5 ounces cotija cheese

lime wedges

*These fresh and flavorful tacos could not be any easier to make. In several of the kitchens where I worked as a pastry chef, a number of my colleagues were expert taco makers. They surely educated this north-of-the-border cook.*

*Make pico de gallo:*

Toss all ingredients in a medium bowl and place in refrigerator.

*Make tacos:*

Char the tortillas over an open flame. Wrap them in aluminum foil to keep warm while you fry the eggs.

Melt 2 tablespoons butter in a large sauté pan over medium heat and add 3 eggs with space between. Reduce heat to low, break the yolks, cover, and cook for 2 minutes. Carefully flip over the eggs with a spatula, cook for 10 seconds, and transfer eggs to a plate. Repeat step to cook the three remaining eggs.

Lay out the tortillas and place an egg on each one. Top with some crumbled cotija cheese and pico de gallo. Fold tacos and serve with lime wedges.

# STUFFED QUICHE

MAKES ONE 9½-INCH QUICHE

### Crust:
1¼ cups all-purpose flour
½ teaspoon salt
½ teaspoon sugar
4 ounces unsalted butter, cold and cubed
3 tablespoons ice water

### Filling:
4 strips of oven-baked crispy bacon (see recipe on page 159)
1 small yellow onion
1 red bell pepper
2 tablespoons olive oil
8 ounces (about 6 medium) brown mushrooms, thinly sliced
7 ounces grated Swiss cheese
¼ cup chives, finely chopped

### Custard:
3 large eggs
¾ cup half-and-half
½ teaspoon salt
¼ teaspoon ground pepper

*My first quiche memory is gingerly making a spinach and bacon quiche in the tiny galley kitchen of my Manhattan studio. Since then, I've made many types of quiche, experimenting with different fillings as I go. Here, I've taken my favorite ingredients and used them all in one recipe. This quiche is stuffed with bacon, onions, red bell peppers, mushrooms, and Swiss cheese. It's incredibly satisfying and delicious!*

*Make crust:*
Combine the flour, salt, and sugar in a mixing bowl with the paddle attachment. Add the cubed butter and mix on medium speed until pea size. Add the water and mix just until dough starts coming together. Gather into a ball with your hands, transfer to a floured surface, and form into a disc. Roll out to a 12-inch round and line the pie tin. Trim and flute the edges, prick holes in the dough with a fork, and place in refrigerator to chill. (Note: If it's a warm day, chill the dough for 10 minutes in the refrigerator before rolling out.)

*Make filling:*
Cook the bacon as directed on page 159. Set aside to cool. Reduce oven to 350°F. Place a sheet tray on center rack. You will bake the quiche on this tray.

Small dice the onion and red pepper. In a large sauté pan, warm the oil over medium heat. Add the onion, pepper, and mushrooms and cook for 8 minutes, stirring occasionally. Remove from heat and set aside. If necessary, drain and dispose of any excess liquid from pan after cooking.

Remove pie shell from refrigerator and bake for 10 minutes. Add a thin layer of the grated cheese to the bottom of the pie shell and bake for 2 minutes more until cheese is melted. Remove from oven and add half of the onion mixture to the pie shell, followed by

*Continued on page 123*

BEACH HOUSE BRUNCH
★ 122 ★

half of the remaining cheese. Chop the bacon into bits and add to pie shell. Top with the remaining onion mixture and cheese. Sprinkle the chopped chives on top.

*Make custard:*
Whisk the eggs, half-and-half, salt, and pepper in a medium bowl and slowly pour the mixture into the pie shell. Bake for 40 minutes, or until an inserted knife comes out clean.

# Eggs San Clemente

## Makes 4 servings

**Potato Pancake:**

1 pound Yukon gold potatoes, washed and dried

½ small yellow onion

1 large egg

⅓ cup breadcrumbs

½ teaspoon salt

½ teaspoon creole seasoning

⅛ teaspoon ground pepper

½ cup peanut or canola oil for frying

**San Clemente:**

½ pound Black Forest Ham, thinly sliced

2 vine ripe tomatoes, sliced about ¼-inch thick

2 large avocados, thinly sliced

8 large eggs

salt and pepper

*San Clemente, California, is the charming beach town that is home to my bakery Sugar Blossom. The weather here is almost always sunny, which allows me to spend much of my free time outside and often at the beach. So, you can imagine that staying fit is important to me. Part of that regimen includes eating healthy whenever possible. In this dish, I replace the typical calorie-laden Hollandaise sauce with the runny yolk of a poached egg and creamy avocado. It's all the sauce you need in this delicious remake of the classic Benedict.*

Medium grate the potatoes in a large bowl. Small grate the onion. Squeeze out the water from the potatoes and onion with your hands over the sink and transfer into a clean, dry bowl.

Mix in the egg, breadcrumbs, salt, creole seasoning, and pepper with your hands until combined. Form 8 patties (about 3 tablespoons each) with your hands and place on a plate.

Preheat oven to 200°F. Warm the oil in a large sauté pan over high heat. (You want the oil to sizzle when you add the potatoes.) Add 4 cakes to the pan and fry 3 minutes per side until golden brown and crispy. Drain on a wire rack over some paper towels. Cook remaining cakes. Place the wire rack (with the cakes) in the oven to keep warm.

Poach the eggs as directed on page 108.

Warm the ham slices in a large sauté pan over high heat for a minute. Lay a few slices over each potato cake and top with a tomato slice and some avocado. Top with poached eggs and serve immediately.

# EGGS WELLINGTON

MAKES 6 SERVINGS

*This dish is one of my favorites to make for brunch. You can prep it the night before and bake it the next morning when guests arrive. Inspired by the classic Beef Wellington, this delicious puff pastry pocket incorporates fluffy scrambled eggs, roast beef, and a delicious layer of crimini and shallots.*

1 (17.3-ounce) package frozen puff pastry sheets

4 tablespoons unsalted butter

6 ounces crimini mushrooms, thinly sliced

1 large shallot, minced

2 garlic cloves, minced

¼ teaspoon salt

⅛ teaspoon pepper

7 large eggs

¼ teaspoon salt

⅛ teaspoon pepper

¼ cup chopped parsley

4 ounces deli roast beef, thinly sliced

3 ounces deli Swiss cheese, thinly sliced

Open the puff pastry package and place the two frozen pastry sheets in the refrigerator to thaw.

Add 2 tablespoons of butter to a large sauté pan and melt over high heat. Add the mushrooms, shallot, garlic, salt, and pepper. Sauté for 5 minutes, transfer to a bowl, and place in refrigerator to cool.

In the same sauté pan, melt the remaining butter over medium heat. Whisk the eggs in a large bowl and reserve 2 tablespoons in a small cup for later. Whisk in the salt and pepper and pour eggs into pan. Gently push, lift, and fold them from one side of the pan to the other until they are nicely clumped, shiny and wet, about 2 minutes. Remove from heat and fold in the parsley. Transfer the eggs to a large plate and refrigerate until cool, about 15 minutes.

Remove one pastry sheet from refrigerator and gently unfold onto a lightly floured surface. Smooth out the creases with your fingers or rolling pin. Transfer the pastry to a foil-lined baking sheet and brush the top with some of the egg wash. Layer the roast beef on top, leaving a 1-inch border. Top with the mushroom mixture, followed by the eggs. Lay the Swiss cheese on top.

Roll out the remaining pastry sheet on a lightly floured surface to extend ½ inch wider on all sides. Lay it over the filling and press down the edges to seal. Use a fork to further seal the edges. Place in the refrigerator to chill for 15 minutes.

Preheat oven to 400°F. Brush the top of the pastry with the remaining egg wash. Bake 30 minutes. Let sit 5 minutes before slicing.

*I recommend using Pepperidge Farm frozen puff pastry sheets.*

# SOUTHWEST SCRAMBLE

MAKES 4 SERVINGS

1 (15-ounce) can black beans

2 plum tomatoes

1 medium jalapeño pepper

¼ cup onion, minced

2 garlic cloves, minced

2 tablespoons unsalted butter

6 large eggs

½ teaspoon salt

¼ teaspoon pepper

5 ounces tortilla chips

1 cup extra sharp cheddar, shredded

¼ cup cilantro, chopped

*This scramble has a great combination of crunchiness, creaminess, and spiciness. The heat of the jalapeños, the warm velvety scrambled eggs, and the crunch of the tortillas are a delicious way to wake up your taste buds in the morning. It's a one pan breakfast meal sure to quell those morning hunger pangs.*

Empty the black beans into a colander and rinse with water. Set aside to drain.

Cut each tomato into 8 wedges and place in a large bowl. Thinly slice the pepper and add to the tomatoes, followed by the minced onion and garlic. Set aside.

Melt the butter in a large sauté pan over medium heat. Whisk the eggs, salt, and pepper in a large bowl and add to the pan. Let the eggs cook undisturbed until the bottom begins to set. Use a rubber spatula to push the eggs toward the center, allowing the uncooked egg to fill the empty space. Continue to move the eggs in this manner until they begin to clump together but are still wet. Add the drained beans, tomato mixture, chips, and half of the shredded cheese to the eggs and gently fold them in. Cover and let simmer over low heat for 5 minutes, stirring occasionally. Remove from heat, top with the remaining cheese, and cilantro. Cover and let sit for 1 minute before serving.

# Foods You Flip

Finding dishes that are both fun to make and eat is doubly wonderful—and this chapter holds a number of these gems. These sweet and savory dishes combine deliciousness with impressive air time (during the flip). The fun you can have while you attempt to flip the food requires only an adventurous spirit and a sound sense of humor. Believe me, the elation you will feel after mastering this skill and showing it off to your friends is worth every missed landing. With these dishes, you can entertain your crowd while creating some wonderful tastes for them—tastes that your guests are sure to flip out over.

# Bananas Foster Pancakes

Makes 4–6 servings, or about 20 pancakes

*Vanilla Sauce:*

12 ounces whole milk

4 ounces heavy cream

6 ounces sugar

1 large vanilla bean, split lengthwise

5 large egg yolks

*Pancakes:*

2 cups all-purpose flour

2 tablespoons sugar

4 teaspoons baking powder

½ teaspoon salt

2 large eggs

1 cup whole milk

½ cup water

4 tablespoons unsalted butter, melted and cooled

*Rum Sauce:*

½ cup dark brown sugar

¼ cup unsalted butter, soft

2 large bananas, ripe

¼ cup dark rum

*When you need to impress, this is the dish to make. Choose yellow bananas that are not too ripe since they need to hold up when cooking. Making the vanilla sauce the night before makes this dish a breeze.*

*Make vanilla sauce:*

In a medium pot, add the milk, cream, and half the sugar. Scrape the vanilla bean halves and add them to the liquid. Bring to a boil over high heat. Meanwhile, whisk the remaining sugar with the egg yolks in a large bowl. Add half the boiling milk mixture into the yolk mixture and whisk well. Pour this mixture back into the pot and return to medium heat, stirring constantly using a rubber spatula. Cook until thickened but not boiling. Set aside. (I like to pour the sauce into squeeze bottles at this point to make for easy plating later.)

*Make pancakes:*

In a large bowl, whisk together the flour, sugar, baking powder, and salt. In a separate bowl, whisk the eggs, milk, water, and melted butter. Add to the dry ingredients and briskly fold in with a rubber spatula just until moistened. Lumps are okay.

Heat a griddle or a nonstick skillet over medium heat. Ladle ¼ cup of batter onto the griddle. Cook for a couple minutes or until bubbles appear on the surface. Flip and cook for another minute. Repeat with remaining batter.

*Make rum sauce:*

Combine the brown sugar and butter in a large sauté pan over medium heat and cook until sugar dissolves. Meanwhile, slice the bananas into coins and add them to the sugar mixture. Coat them with the sauce and, when the bananas soften slightly, carefully pour in the rum. Continue to cook the sauce until the rum is hot and bananas are nicely browned, then ignite the rum with a hand-held lighter. When the flames subside, remove from heat.

*Plating:*

Layer a stack of pancakes with some vanilla sauce between each pancake. Top with some bananas, followed by the rum sauce and more vanilla sauce. Serve immediately.

# BLUEBERRY WHOLE WHEAT PANCAKES
# WITH SALTED BUTTER

MAKES 10 LARGE PANCAKES

*I love a dish that tastes too good to be healthy but is. In these scrumptious pancakes lies a perfect balance of sweet from the blueberries, nuttiness from the wheat, tang from buttermilk, and saltiness from the butter. They all blend into something mightily delicious and deceptively nutritious!*

In a medium bowl, slightly mash the blueberries and 2 tablespoons sugar with a fork. Set aside.

In a large bowl, whisk together the buttermilk, eggs, remaining sugar, butter, and vanilla. Stir in the blueberry mixture with a rubber spatula. Mix in the flour, baking powder, and baking soda until combined. Batter will be thick.

Heat a griddle or a nonstick skillet. Ladle ½ cup of batter onto the griddle. Spread out the batter, if necessary. Cook for a couple minutes or until bubbles appear on the surface. Flip and cook for another minute. Repeat with remaining batter. Serve warm with salted butter and maple syrup.

2 cups fresh blueberries

6 tablespoons sugar

1½ cups buttermilk

2 large eggs

4 tablespoons unsalted butter, melted

1 teaspoon pure vanilla extract

2 cups whole wheat flour

1 teaspoon baking powder

½ teaspoon baking soda

salted butter and maple syrup, for serving

# CRANBERRY WALNUT FRENCH TOAST

MAKES 2–3 SERVINGS

1 (12-ounce) "take & bake" La Brea Bakery cranberry walnut loaf, <u>baked the night before</u>

3 tablespoons sugar

½ teaspoon ground cinnamon

3 large eggs

2 tablespoons half-and-half

4 tablespoons unsalted butter

maple syrup and powdered sugar, for serving

*This recipe uses La Brea Bakery's "take & bake" cranberry walnut loaf, which can be found at most grocery stores. Be sure to bake it the night before so it's completely cool the next morning. The custard's ratio of egg, sugar, and cream strikes the ideal balance—neither too wet and soggy nor too firm and eggy.*

Preheat oven to 200°F. Place a sheet tray on the center rack.

Using a serrated knife, cut the pre-baked loaf into 1-inch-thick slices (save the end pieces for snacking later in the day).

In a medium bowl, whisk together the sugar and cinnamon. Whisk in the eggs, followed by the half-and-half. Transfer mixture to a large, shallow plate.

Heat 2 tablespoons of butter in a 12-inch nonstick skillet over medium-high heat until foam subsides. Soak the bread slices in the egg mixture, turning over once, until saturated. Transfer the soaked bread slices with a slotted spatula to the skillet and cook, turning once, until golden brown on each side, about 3 minutes total. Transfer to the sheet tray and keep warm in oven. Soak the rest of the bread slices and cook with the remaining butter. Serve warm with maple syrup and powdered sugar.

# CREAMY CHICKEN CREPES

MAKES ABOUT 5 SERVINGS

*These neatly packaged crepes are filled with tender chicken and a mouthwatering creamy Madeira sauce. In fact, I often double the sauce so I can enjoy it on its own with a baguette the next day. The lovely presentation of this dish makes this recipe suitable for more formal brunches.*

**Crepes:**

1 cup whole milk

1 large egg

2 tablespoons sugar

1 tablespoon unsalted butter, melted

¼ teaspoon salt

1 cup all-purpose flour

**Chicken Filling:**

1 pound chicken breasts, skinless

1 tablespoon cornstarch

1 teaspoon salt

½ teaspoon pepper

½ teaspoon onion powder

1 tablespoon olive oil

2 tablespoons unsalted butter, soft

1 large shallot, minced

2 garlic cloves, minced

½ cup Madeira

½ cup heavy cream

¼ cup sour cream

2 tablespoons chopped chives

extra chives, for wrapping

*Make crepes:*
Add all ingredients in the order listed to a blender. Mix just until combined, about 6 seconds. Strain into a bain-marie or bowl. Let batter rest in refrigerator 30 minutes.

Heat a nonstick 8-inch skillet over medium heat. Add ¼ cup of batter to the pan and swirl the pan in a continuous circular motion until evenly spread. Let cook until edges start to turn light brown and curl upward, about 90 seconds. Use a dinner knife to lift up one edge and use your fingers to flip over crepe. Cook for 30 seconds. Transfer to a plate. Stack up crepes as you make them. Wrap with foil to keep warm.

*Make chicken filling:*
Medium dice the chicken breasts and add to a large bowl. Mix in the cornstarch, salt, pepper, and onion powder. Add the oil to a large sauté pan over high heat. Add the chicken and stir occasionally until cooked through, about 10 minutes. Transfer chicken to a plate and set aside.

Add the butter to the sauté pan and cook the shallots and garlic for 2 minutes over high heat. Add the Madeira and reduce by half, about 2 minutes. Whisk in the heavy cream and sour cream. Stir in the chicken along with any juices. Continue to boil until sauce thickens, about 3 minutes. Remove from heat and stir in the chopped chives.

*Wrap crepes:*
Turn oven on to 250°F. Line a sheet tray with aluminum foil and set aside.

On a flat, clean surface, lay out the crepes. Place about ½ cup of the chicken filling in the center of each crepe. Bring ends up and tie with a single chive. Transfer them to the prepared sheet tray. Place crepes in oven for 5 minutes to reheat before serving.

# Baked Prosciutto Crepes in Blue Cheese Sauce

Makes about 5 servings

*These savory crepes are hugely satisfying and are baked in a rich, bubbling blue cheese sauce. To save time, you can assemble the crepes in the baking pan and keep them covered in the refrigerator until you make the sauce. Serve these crepes straight out of the oven.*

### Make crepes:

Add all ingredients in the order listed to a blender. Mix just until combined, about 6 seconds. Strain into a bain-marie or bowl. Let batter rest in refrigerator 30 minutes.

Heat a nonstick 8-inch skillet over medium heat. Add ¼ cup of batter to the pan and swirl the pan in a continuous circular motion until evenly spread. Let cook until edges start to turn light brown and curl upward, about 90 seconds. Use a dinner knife to lift up one edge and use your hands to flip over crepe. Cook for 30 seconds. Transfer to a plate. Stack up crepes as you make them. Wrap with foil to keep warm.

### Make filling:

Coat the bottom of a 13 × 9-inch baking pan with the butter and set aside. Preheat broiler to high. Toss the asparagus in a bowl with olive oil and salt. Spread onto foil-lined sheet tray and broil for 8 to 10 minutes until they are al dente. Remove from oven and set aside. Adjust oven to 350°F.

On a flat, clean surface, lay out the crepes. Spread a couple teaspoons of fig preserves down the center of each crepe. Lay a couple strips of prosciutto on top followed by a few asparagus spears. Roll up each crepe and place in the prepared pan.

### Make blue cheese sauce:

Melt the butter in a medium pot over high heat. Add the garlic and shallots. Cook until soft, about 2 minutes. Stir in the flour and cook for 1 minute until tan in color. Warm the milk and broth in the microwave and slowly stir them into the flour mixture. Add the salt and pepper. Continue cooking for 5 minutes until thickened, stirring occasionally. Add the cheese and cook for another minute, whisking until smooth. Pour over the crepes. Bake for 15 minutes. Serve warm.

## Crepes:

- 1 cup whole milk
- 1 large egg
- 2 tablespoons sugar
- 1 tablespoon unsalted butter, melted
- ¼ teaspoon salt
- 1 cup all-purpose flour

## Filling:

- 2 tablespoons unsalted butter, soft
- 1 bunch asparagus, trimmed and cleaned
- 1 teaspoon olive oil
- ¼ teaspoon salt
- ½ cup fig preserves
- ½ pound prosciutto, thinly sliced

## Blue Cheese Sauce:

- 2 tablespoons unsalted butter
- 2 garlic clove, minced
- 1 tablespoon minced shallots
- 2 tablespoons all-purpose flour
- 1½ cups low-fat milk
- 1 cup chicken broth
- ¼ teaspoon salt
- ⅛ teaspoon pepper
- 4 ounces blue cheese, crumbled

# Chocolate Tiramisu Crepes

*Chocolate Crepes:*
1 cup whole milk
2 large eggs
¼ cup sugar
2 tablespoons unsalted butter, melted
¼ teaspoon salt
¾ cup all-purpose flour
¼ cup cocoa powder

*Mascarpone Filling:*
1 (8-ounce) container mascarpone cheese
½ cup powdered sugar, sifted
2 tablespoons coffee-flavored liqueur (such as Copa De Oro)

*Chocolate Sauce:*
1 cup heavy cream
9 ounces dark chocolate chips

*Vanilla Whipped Cream:*
1 cup heavy cream
2 tablespoons sugar
1 teaspoon pure vanilla extract

*Garnishes:*
½ cup powdered sugar
1 Hershey's chocolate bar
Fresh berries

*These dessert crepes are always a welcome sight after any meal. Who can resist a chocolatey crepe filled with coffee-spiked mascarpone drizzled with chocolate sauce and topped with fresh berries?*

*Make chocolate crepes:*
Add all ingredients in the order listed to a blender. Mix just until combined, about 6 seconds. Strain into a bain-marie or bowl. Let batter rest in refrigerator 30 minutes.

Heat a nonstick 8-inch skillet over medium heat. Add ¼ cup of batter to the pan and swirl the pan in a continuous circular motion until evenly spread. Let cook until edges start to curl upward, about 90 seconds. Use a small rubber spatula to lift up one edge and use your fingers to flip crepe over. Cook for 30 seconds. Transfer to a plate. Stack up crepes as you make them.

*Make mascarpone filling and chocolate sauce:*
In a medium bowl, whisk the mascarpone, sugar, and liqueur until incorporated. Set aside. In a small pot, bring the cream to just a boil over medium heat. Remove from heat and add the chocolate chips. Whisk until smooth. Set aside.

*Make vanilla whipped cream:*
In a stand mixer with the whip attachment, mix the heavy cream, sugar, and vanilla on high speed until stiff peaks form. Transfer to a piping bag with a star tip and place in refrigerator.

*Fill crepes:*
Spread a thin layer of mascarpone filling over each crepe. Roll up or fold in quarters and place a few on a plate or in a parchment cone. Garnish with chocolate sauce, whipped cream, and sifted powdered sugar. Use a microplane to grate the chocolate over the crepes and finish with some fresh berries.

# MAPLE PECAN WAFFLES

*The candied pecans in the waffle batter provide a nice texture to an otherwise normal morning dish. Every bite of this sweet brunch dish gets better and better as the waffles soak up every bit of the warm maple butter syrup.*

## Candied Pecans:
- 1 egg white
- 1 teaspoon water
- 1 cup pecan pieces
- ¼ cup sugar
- ½ teaspoon ground cinnamon

## Vanilla Whipped Cream:
- 1 cup heavy cream
- 2 tablespoons sugar
- 1 teaspoon pure vanilla extract

## Waffles:
- 2 large eggs, separated
- ¾ cup whole milk
- ¼ cup vegetable oil
- 1 teaspoon pure vanilla extract
- 1 cup all-purpose flour
- 2 tablespoons sugar
- 1 teaspoon baking powder
- ¼ teaspoon ground cinnamon
- ¼ teaspoon salt
- 3 tablespoons unsalted butter, soft
- ½ cup maple syrup

*Make candied pecans (the night before):*
Preheat oven to 250°F. Line a sheet tray with aluminum foil or parchment. Whisk the egg white and water in a small bowl. Stir in the pecans until well-coated. Add the sugar and cinnamon to the pecans and coat well. Transfer to the prepared sheet tray spread out with a fork. Bake for 60 minutes, stirring every 15 minutes. Let cool on counter overnight.

*Make vanilla whipped cream:*
In a mixing bowl with the whip attachment, mix the heavy cream, sugar, and vanilla on high speed to soft peaks. Place in refrigerator until needed.

*Make waffles:*
Preheat oven to 200°F and turn on waffle maker. In a mixing bowl with the whip attachment, beat the 2 egg whites to stiff peak and transfer to a clean bowl.

In the same bowl, whip together the egg yolks, milk, oil, and vanilla until combined. Add the flour, sugar, baking powder, cinnamon, and salt. Mix until incorporated. Remove bowl from mixer and fold in half of the pecans, followed by the egg whites.

Cook batter immediately in waffle maker (I cook mine for about 4 minutes). Remove waffles and place in oven, directly on the racks to keep warm. Continue cooking remaining batter.

In a small pot, preferably with a lip, melt the butter over low heat. Stir in the maple syrup and heat until warmed through. Pour a little of the syrup on each serving plate and place a stack of waffles on top. Top with additional syrup, whipped cream, and candied pecans.

*Ultimate Corned Beef Hash*

# Hashes

Hashes bring substance and a certain "meatiness" to a meal, even if they're free of actual meat. If you feel like your brunch menu needs a dish with some gravitas, then look no further than hashes; they're wonderfully filling without the fuss. In fact, most of the time, you can pull together a hash with what's already in your refrigerator. You can even use the recipes in this chapter as a guide and substitute or add ingredients as you desire. In this chapter, you'll find the classic Corned Beef Hash and my Ten Veggie Hash, which even a carnivore will love. I trust you'll find these recipes reliable and will decide to add them to your brunch menu when an impact is desired.

# ULTIMATE CORNED BEEF HASH

MAKES 5–6 SERVINGS

2 pounds corned beef, <u>cooked</u>

1 pound Yukon gold potatoes, medium diced

½ cup unsalted butter, soft

1 medium yellow onion, small diced

2 teaspoons salt

1 teaspoon ground pepper

½ cup fresh parsley or scallions, chopped

*The trick to making this ultimate hash is letting it cook undisturbed so the meat caramelizes and chars. I use a higher ratio of corned beef to potatoes, as I prefer a meatier hash.*

Bring 8 cups of water to a boil over high heat. While the water comes to a boil, shred or medium dice the corned beef, place in a large bowl, and set aside.

Add the diced potatoes and pinch of salt to the boiling water and cook for 5 minutes. Strain well, blot them dry with a paper towel, and toss them in with the corned beef.

Melt butter in a 12-inch cast iron skillet over medium-high heat. Add the onions and cook for 3 to 4 minutes, stirring occasionally. Add the beef and potato mixture, followed by salt and pepper. Press down with the back of spatula to flatten like a pancake. Cover with a large, round pizza tray or foil. Cook undisturbed until bottom is golden brown, about 5 minutes. Using a spatula, flip the hash in portions and flatten again. Cover and cook for another 5 minutes. Transfer to plates and garnish with chopped fresh parsley or scallions. Serve with any style eggs.

# SCALLION HASH BROWNS

MAKES ONE 10-INCH ROUND

*These crispy, delicious hash browns with creamy centers are always a crowd pleaser. They pair well with any style of eggs. Make sure to remove as much juice from the potatoes as you can to ensure their crispiness.*

- 3 medium Yukon gold potatoes
- 4 large scallions, thinly sliced
- 2 cloves garlic, minced
- ¼ teaspoon salt
- ⅛ teaspoon pepper
- ½ cup olive oil

Wash and dry the potatoes well. Grate them into a bowl and firmly squeeze the shreds with your hands over a sink to remove the juices. Spread them onto a double-folded paper towel and press down with another paper towel to release any excess juice. The more juice you get out, the crispier the hash browns will be. Return the shreds to the bowl (make sure the bowl is dry) and mix in the scallions, garlic, salt, and pepper.

Warm half the olive oil in a 10-inch sauté pan over high heat. Add the potato mixture and spread it out as evenly as possible on the bottom, careful to not go up the sides. (I like to use the bottom of a cup to flatten it out.) Cook for 5 minutes undisturbed. Place a flat plate or cutting board on top of the pan and flip out. Add the remaining oil to the pan. Slide the hash brown back into the sauté pan. Cook for 5 minutes undisturbed. Sprinkle with a dash of salt and serve warm.

# TEN VEGGIE HASH

*This veggie-packed hash has the comforting flavors of sage and parsley. The white corn, kale, and squash are a nice change from popular meat and potato hashes.*

Wash and dry potato well. On a cutting board with a sharp knife, small dice the potato and transfer to a large bowl.

Cut off the ends of the squash. Peel off the skin and discard. Cut the squash in half where the neck and body meet. Cut the neck half into ½-inch-thick rings and then proceed to cut ½-inch-thick cubes from each ring. Add to the potatoes. Cut the body section in half lengthwise and remove the seeds. Slice each half into ½-inch strips and each strip into ½-inch cubes. Add to the bowl.

Remove the stem and seeds from the red pepper and cut into ½-inch cubes. Combine the cubes with the potato. Add the mushrooms to the bowl.

Warm the oil and butter in a medium stockpot over high heat. Add the garlic and shallot and cook for 30 seconds. Add the vegetable mixture, salt, and pepper. Cover and let cook for about 7 minutes, stirring occasionally.

Meanwhile, slice the kernels from the corn and place in a large bowl. Chiffonade the kale leaves and add to the corn. Stir in the parsley and sage. Add mixture to the stockpot. Cover and cook for another 3 minutes, stirring occasionally. Remove from heat. Let rest 5 minutes. Top with grated parmesan before serving.

1 large Yukon gold potato

1 butternut squash

1 red bell pepper

5 ounces shiitake mushrooms, thinly sliced

2 tablespoons olive oil

2 tablespoons unsalted butter

2 garlic cloves, minced

1 large shallot, minced

1 teaspoon salt

½ teaspoon pepper

2 ears of white corn, shucked

1 bunch curly green kale, stems trimmed

¼ cup Italian parsley, chopped

2 tablespoons fresh sage, chopped

grated parmesan cheese, for serving

# Skillet Home Fries

2 tablespoons unsalted butter, soft

2 tablespoons olive oil

¼ cup yellow onion, thinly sliced

2 cloves garlic, minced

1 serrano chili, thinly sliced

2 large Yukon gold potatoes, small diced with skin on

¼ teaspoon salt

⅛ teaspoon ground pepper

*The addition of serrano chili in these home fries adds just the right amount of kick to liven up your morning routine. Don't need the kick but want the flavor? Simply remove the chili seeds before slicing.*

Melt the butter and olive oil over medium heat in a large skillet. Add the onion and sauté until translucent, about 2 minutes. Add the garlic and chili; sauté another minute. Stir in the diced potatoes, salt, and pepper. Flatten potato mixture into an even layer. Cover with lid and cook until potatoes are cooked through, about 8 minutes. Stir occasionally to prevent sticking. Serve warm.

# HEAVENLY HASH

MAKES 4 SERVINGS

1 large Yukon gold
potato

canola oil and salt

4 strips of bacon

1 tablespoon unsalted
butter

1 tablespoon olive oil

½ medium yellow on-
ion, diced

½ bunch curly green
kale, stems trimmed

¼ teaspoon salt

⅛ teaspoon pepper

1 cup sharp cheddar
cheese, grated

*There's a great little breakfast spot down the street from the beach house at Dana Point Harbor. It's a wood and glass building steps away from the marina where locals love to gather every morning for warm, delicious, and reasonably priced breakfast fare. Vast outdoor patio seating is available with sailboats anchored nearby. This hash is my take on one of their most popular dishes.*

Preheat oven to 350°F. Wash the potato under cold running water with a stiff brush. Dry thoroughly with paper towels. Poke holes in the potato with a fork. Coat with canola oil and salt. Place directly onto middle oven rack. Place a foil-lined sheet tray on the bottom rack to catch drippings. Bake 1 hour or until skin feels crisp but flesh beneath feels soft. Remove from oven and set out on counter to cool.

Cook the bacon as directed on page 159. Set aside.

Heat the butter and olive oil in a sauté pan over medium heat. Add the onions and cook until they start to caramelize, about eight minutes. Roll up the kale leaves and chiffonade them. Add them to the pan and cook for five minutes, stirring occasionally. Rough cut the baked potato into small cubes. Cut the bacon into bits. Add them to the sauté pan along with the salt and pepper. Cover and let cook until warmed through, about 5 minutes. Remove from heat and gently stir in half the cheese. Top with the remaining cheese, cover, and let sit for 2 minutes before serving.

# Surf-n-Go

Breakfast may be the most important meal of the day, but it can also be the hardest to make time for on very busy days—or on days when you're running way later than expected. Sometimes we just don't have enough time to stick around in the morning for a sit-down breakfast or brunch. When I have guests who are short on time, I whip out these recipes and have everything ready to hand them on their way out the door. Even if you don't have a surfboard on the top of your vehicle or the ocean is too far away for a quick trip, having some go-to favorites that satisfy hunger and put a smile on the faces of those you care about will make you feel like you've ridden a beautiful wave all the way into shore. Just step off the board, bid farewell to the happy crowd, and acknowledge the applause.

# LOADED BURRITOS

2 medium Yukon gold potatoes

canola oil and salt

6 strips bacon

2 tablespoons unsalted butter, melted

1 tablespoon olive oil

½ cup yellow onion, small diced

2 cups baby arugula

4 large eggs

½ cup sharp cheddar, grated

salt and pepper to taste

tabasco sauce, optional

2 large soft flour tortillas

*Who doesn't love a fat, warm burrito in the morning? I load up mine with potatoes, eggs, bacon, arugula, and cheddar. Wrap it up in foil and you've got the perfect breakfast on the run. Make sure to plan ahead and bake the potatoes the night before.*

*The night before:*
Preheat oven to 350°F. Wash the potatoes under cold running water with a stiff brush. Dry thoroughly with paper towels. Poke holes in the potatoes with a fork. Coat the potatoes with canola oil and salt in a large bowl. Place potatoes directly onto middle oven rack. Place a foil-lined sheet tray on the bottom rack to catch drippings. Bake 1 hour or until skin feels crisp but flesh beneath feels soft. Remove from oven and place in refrigerator to cool overnight.

*The next morning:*
Cook the bacon as directed on page 159. Set aside.

Medium dice the potatoes and set aside. In a large sauté pan over medium heat, melt 1 tablespoon butter and the oil. Add the onions and cook until translucent. Add the potatoes to pan and spread them out to one layer. Let potatoes crisp slightly, turning occasionally to crisp up all sides. Chop the crispy bacon into bits and add to the pan with the arugula. Mix in until arugula has wilted. Push potato mixture off to one side and reduce heat to low. Add the remaining tablespoon of butter to the exposed surface and add the four eggs. Season the eggs with a little salt and stir the eggs briskly with a rubber spatula to break up yolks. Continue stirring the eggs occasionally to scramble them. When eggs begin to dry, stir them in with the potato mixture and add the cheese. Continue mixing until cheese starts to melt. Remove from heat and add salt and pepper to taste.

Divide the mixture between the two flour tortillas. Sprinkle tabasco sauce on top of filling, if desired. Roll burritos tight and slice in half. Serve warm.

## Oven-Baked Crispy Bacon

I don't know about you, but one of my favorite breakfasts on the run is crispy bacon. Its protein and saltiness satisfy my hunger pangs immediately. I've found that cooking bacon in the oven is the best and easiest way to prepare it with minimal effort. The bacon fries in its own grease, making it crispy and oh-so-tasty. Best part of it all? It's a breeze to clean up afterward because all you need is a rimmed baking tray and a sheet of aluminum foil.

⋆ ⋆

Preheat oven to 385°F. Line a sheet tray including the edges with aluminum foil. If it's a flat tray, fold up the four sides of the foil to create a ½-inch tall barrier. Lay strips of bacon on the tray in a single layer with some space between. Bake until bacon is browned and crispy, about 18 to 20 minutes. Transfer the bacon to a plate lined with paper towels to drain grease. Serve warm.

Set aside tray until completely cooled. Roll up aluminum foil and discard.

# GRILLED STEAK, EGGS, AND TRUFFLE CHEESE QUESADILLA

MAKES 2 LARGE QUESADILLAS

*Grilled Steak:*

2 tablespoons rosemary leaves

8 garlic cloves

1 large shallot, roughly chopped

1 cup olive oil

1 pound rib eye

salt and pepper

*Filling:*

4 tablespoons unsalted butter

1 small sweet onion, diced

1 teaspoon sugar

¼ teaspoon salt

7 large eggs

6 large flour tortillas

2 cups Italian truffle cheese, shredded

*I recommend using Trader Joe's Italian Truffle Cheese.*

*This multi-layered, mouthwatering quesadilla is always a crowd pleaser. It's stuffed with juicy steak marinated in rosemary, garlic, and shallots. Caramelized onions, creamy scrambled eggs, and truffle cheese are layered between the tortillas, making this quesadilla unforgettable.*

*Make grilled steak:*

Combine the rosemary, garlic, shallot, and oil in a blender and purée until smooth. Place steak in a large zip top bag. Pour the marinade over the steak, seal the bag, and massage the marinade into the meat. Lay flat in the refrigerator for at least 1 hour.

Preheat your grill with moderate heat. Remove steak from bag, discard any excess marinade, and season with salt and pepper. Grill the steak to medium rare, about 3 minutes per side. Transfer steak to a cutting board and let rest.

*Make filling:*

In a large sauté pan, melt 1 tablespoon butter over medium heat. Add the onion, sugar, and salt. Cook until onions become caramelized, stirring frequently, about 10 minutes. Transfer to a small bowl and set aside.

Return pan to medium heat and melt a tablespoon of butter. Lightly whisk the eggs and a pinch of salt together. Pour in the eggs and let it sit, without stirring, for 20 seconds. Stir with a rubber spatula, lifting and folding it over from the bottom of the pan. Let it sit for another 10 seconds then stir and fold again. Repeat until the eggs are softly set and slightly runny in places. Remove from heat, cover, and set aside.

*Continued on page 161*

Thinly slice the steak across the grain. Melt a tablespoon of butter in the sauté pan over low heat. Lay one tortilla down and sprinkle with ¼ cup of cheese, followed by half the caramelized onions, half the steak, and another ¼ cup of cheese.

Lay down another tortilla and top with ¼ cup of cheese and half the eggs. Top with ¼ cup of cheese and another tortilla. Press down firmly, cover skillet, and let cook for 5 minutes. Place a plate on top of the quesadilla and carefully flip the quesadilla onto the plate. Slide it back into the pan and cook the other side for 4 minutes. Transfer to a cutting board and cut into wedges. Repeat step to make second quesadilla.

# Egg Spamwich

## Makes 2 SPAMwiches

2 tablespoons unsalted butter, soft

4 slices Hawaiian sweet bread

2 tablespoons mayonnaise

1 tablespoon sriracha

2 cups cabbage, thinly sliced

1 (12-ounce) can SPAM® classic

2 large eggs

salt and pepper

*A true surf breakfast isn't complete unless there's SPAM® involved. Even those who shun the popular canned meat cannot deny how tasty this SPAMwich is. Packed with veggies and protein, it will give the surfers in your life plenty of energy for their morning rides. I recommend using a panini press for this recipe.*

Evenly spread 1 tablespoon of butter onto one side of each slice of bread. Lay them flat on a cutting board and set aside.

In a medium bowl, stir together the mayonnaise and sriracha. Add the sliced cabbage and stir to coat. Set aside and preheat panini press.

Cut the SPAM® into eight ¼-inch slices. Warm a large nonstick sauté pan over medium heat. Add the meat and cook until golden brown, about 4 minutes per side. Lay two slices of meat onto each piece of bread. Reduce heat to low and melt the remaining butter in the pan. Add the two eggs, poke the yolks, cover, and cook for 3 minutes. Top two of the bread slices with the fried eggs followed by the cabbage and then sandwich them with the two remaining slices of bread. Place the sandwiches in a panini press and cook until golden brown, about 2 minutes. Wrap bottom halves with foil and hand them out to the morning surf crew.

# No-Bake Energy Bars

*Not just for mornings, these flavorful energy bars are great any time of day. I like to keep a bunch in my freezer individually wrapped in foil for surfers or guests who have early morning departures.*

Grease a 6 × 6-inch square pan and set aside.

Heat a small skillet over high heat. Add the raw pecans and toss frequently until fragrant and toasted, about 5 minutes. Transfer pecans to a large stainless steel bowl. Add the oats, cereal, coconut, brown sugar, and salt, and toss to combine. Set aside.

In a small bowl, stir together the peanut butter, honey, and butter. Pour onto the dry ingredients and, using clean hands, mix well until all ingredients are well distributed. Mixture will be sticky.

Transfer to the prepared pan and flatten with a piece of plastic wrap or a zip top bag. Place pan in the freezer for 30 minutes to firm up. When ready, flip the mixture out onto a cutting board and cut into eight bars with a sharp knife. Wrap in foil and store in the refrigerator or freezer for a surf-n-go breakfast.

½ cup raw pecans, finely chopped

1 cup rolled oats

½ cup grape nuts cereal

½ cup coconut, shredded

1 tablespoon light brown sugar

¼ teaspoon salt

½ cup smooth peanut butter

¼ cup orange blossom honey

1 tablespoon unsalted butter, melted

# CRISPY QUINOA PITA POCKET

*These crispy little quinoa cakes make a great vegetarian brunch option. Flavors of Thailand and Greece combine to make a delectable meal. Stuff them in a pita pocket for groms heading out the door. Use the leftovers on a salad for those who are slow to wake.*

*Cucumber Yogurt Sauce:*
1 small cucumber
½ cup Greek yogurt
½ cup sour cream
2 garlic cloves, minced
1 teaspoon dill, chopped
1 teaspoon lemon zest
¼ teaspoon salt
⅛ teaspoon ground pepper

*Quinoa Patties:*
1 cup quinoa, cooked (⅓ cup raw quinoa cooked according to package directions)
¼ cup red onion, minced
2 tablespoons unsalted butter, soft
2 tablespoons parsley, chopped
2 large eggs
½ cup coconut milk
2 teaspoons curry powder
1 teaspoon salt
1 cup black beans, drained and rinsed with water
½ cup bread crumbs
olive oil for pan frying
5– 6 pita halves
frisée or any mixed greens, for garnish

*Make cucumber yogurt sauce:*
Thinly slice the cucumber and place in a medium bowl. Stir in the remaining ingredients and let chill in refrigerator while you make the patties.

*Make quinoa patties:*
Stir together the quinoa, onion, butter, and parsley in a large bowl. Add the eggs, coconut milk, curry powder, and salt. Mix well. Fold in the beans and breadcrumbs. Form into small patties with your hands and place them on a plate.

Warm about 2 tablespoons of olive oil in a skillet over medium heat. (You want the oil to sizzle when you add the patties.) Place several patties in the pan with about ½ inch space between them. Cover and cook until bottoms are golden brown, about 5 to 7 minutes. Flip patties over and cook 5 minutes more, until bottoms are golden brown. Remove from skillet and let rest on wire rack. Add new oil to the pan and cook remaining patties.

Open pitas and stuff them with friseé or any mixed greens and a few patties. Top with the cucumber yogurt sauce.

*I prefer using Persian cucumber for its thinner skin and crispier flesh.*

*Heirloom Cherry Tomato Salad*

# Salads and Casseroles

These salad and casserole recipes are great for brunches that lean more toward the lunch side of brunch, when the sun is higher up in the sky. Many of the salads are excellent served with the savory breads in this book and are delicious for dinner, too. The casseroles are pure comfort food—dishes I love making when it's just the girlfriends or close acquaintances. You may decide to try out these salads on those in your life for whom salads are usually a "pass" at most meals. Don't forget that some of these recipes are intended to change the minds of your guests and family who make a funny face if you suggest a salad or casserole is in their immediate future. Surprise, surprise, they are delicious and you have won their loyalty, allowing you to whip up more adventurous dishes while expanding their food horizons.

# MIXED GREENS SALAD
## WITH CANDIED PECANS, POMEGRANATE, AND FETA

MAKES 4 SERVINGS

*This is a scrumptious salad that goes well with any dish. The lemon garlic dressing is easy to make and pulls together all the flavors remarkably well. If pomegranates are hard to find, orange segments are a nice substitute.*

*Candied Pecans:*
1 tablespoon unsalted butter
2 tablespoons light brown sugar
½ cup raw whole pecans

*Salad:*
5–5.5 ounces washed and dry ⁵⁰⁄₅₀ blend baby spinach and spring mix
½ cup red onions, thinly sliced
3 ounces feta cheese, crumbled
1 pomegranate, seeded

*Make candied pecans:*
Line a sheet tray with aluminum foil. In a small sauté pan over medium heat, melt the butter. Stir in the brown sugar. With mixture bubbling, add the pecans and cook until pecans are toasted and mixture thickens, about 3 minutes. Stir frequently. Transfer candied pecans to prepared tray. Separate nuts with a fork and set aside to cool.

*Make salad:*
Place all ingredients in a large bowl and set aside while you make the dressing.

---

**Lemon Garlic Dressing**

You will need: ¼ cup extra virgin olive oil, 1½ tablespoons fresh lemon juice, 1 clove minced garlic, ¼ teaspoon oregano, ¼ teaspoon salt, ⅛ teaspoon ground pepper.

**Directions:**
Whisk together all ingredients in a small bowl and pour over salad. Toss well and top with the candied pecans. Serve immediately.

# Italian Sausage Casserole

*My goal with this dish was to create a savory version of bread pudding with just a hint of sweetness. Leftover French bread works well in this recipe, but many other types of bread can also be used. This casserole is best served straight out of the oven.*

4 tablespoons unsalted butter, soft
8 ounces French bread, cubed

*Filling:*
5 sweet Italian sausage links, casings removed (about 19 ounces)
1 tablespoon olive oil
¼ cup sweet onion, minced
1 large red bell pepper, small diced
1 large zucchini, cut into ⅛-inch-thick coins
3 large cremini mushrooms, thinly sliced
2 cloves garlic, minced
10 small basil leaves, chiffonade

¼ cup fresh parsley, chopped, plus more for garnish
1 teaspoon dried oregano
1 cup mozzarella cheese, shredded

*Custard:*
1 cup whole milk
1 cup heavy cream
2 tablespoons sugar
3 large eggs
2 large egg yolks

Preheat oven to 350°F. Grease a 13 × 9-inch baking pan with 4 tablespoons butter. Add the cubed bread in one layer and set aside.

*Make filling:*
In a large sauté pan over high heat, thoroughly cook the sausage, about 10 minutes. Use a rubber spatula to break up the sausage and stir occasionally to prevent burning. Transfer the cooked sausage to a paper towel to drain.

In the same sauté pan, warm the olive oil and cook the onions until translucent, about 2 minutes. Add the pepper, zucchini, mushrooms, and garlic. Cook for about 10 minutes, until vegetables soften. Stir in the basil, parsley, and oregano, and cook for an additional minute. Remove from heat.

Spread the cooked sausage over the bread, followed by the vegetable mixture, and top with the cheese. Set aside.

*Continued on page 172*

*Make custard:*

Bring milk, cream, and 1 tablespoon sugar to a boil over high heat and remove from heat. Whisk eggs, yolks, and remaining sugar in a large bowl. Slowly add the hot liquid to the egg mixture while whisking. Pour custard into casserole dish. Press down top of the casserole with the back of a flat spatula to submerge mozzarella layer.

Bake for 30 minutes or until the casserole boils and sets up. Remove from oven and let rest for 10 minutes before serving. Garnish with additional chopped parsley.

# HEIRLOOM CHERRY TOMATO SALAD

MAKES 4–6 SERVINGS

*This is a super flavorful salad to make during the late summer months when heirloom tomatoes are at their peak. It's wonderful served with grilled or broiled salmon.*

Using a sharp knife, cut the tomatoes in half and transfer to a large bowl. Slice the cucumbers into thin coins and add to the bowl. Add the remaining ingredients to the bowl and mix with a spoon until combined. Let chill in the refrigerator for at least 30 minutes before serving.

2 pints heirloom cherry tomatoes
2 medium cucumbers
1 cup green olives, halved
2 garlic cloves, minced
⅓ cup parsley, chopped
¼ cup balsamic vinegar
2 tablespoons shallots, minced
½ teaspoon salt
½ teaspoon ground pepper

*I prefer using Persian cucumber for its thinner and crispier flesh.*

# Asian Slaw

½ cup frying oil such as peanut or canola

15 wonton skins

1 head napa cabbage, thinly sliced

1 red pepper, stem and seeds removed, small diced

3 cups carrots, shredded

3 green onions, thinly sliced

1 cup peanuts, roasted and salted

*This colorful crispy salad boasts a healthy dose of vegetables and a dressing that's big on flavor. The crunchy vegetables and peanuts along with the tang of the dressing bring complexity and layers of taste to what is sometimes a simple side dish.*

Warm oil in medium saucepan over medium heat. Cut wonton skins in ¼-inch strips and fry in two batches until golden brown. Let fried wontons drain on paper towels while you prepare salad.

Combine the cabbage, red pepper, carrots, green onions, and peanuts in a large salad bowl.

---

**Asian Dressing**

You will need: ⅓ cup soy sauce, ¼ cup extra virgin olive oil, 2 tablespoons mirin, 1 tablespoon rice wine vinegar, 1 teaspoon sesame oil, 1-inch peeled and minced fresh ginger, and 2 cloves minced garlic.

**Directions:**
In a separate bowl, whisk together all the dressing ingredients. Pour over vegetables and toss well. Garnish with fried wontons. Serve immediately.

# LAYERED SPINACH SALAD

*This salad is packed with protein and carbs that make it a meal on its own. If building this salad ahead of time, add the bacon and parmesan toppings right before serving. I like to serve this salad in a glass trifle dish to showcase all the layers.*

6 strips of oven-baked crispy bacon (see page 159 for recipe)

8 large hard-boiled eggs (see page 105 for recipe)

*Salad:*

5–5.5 ounces baby spinach

1 (14-ounce) can artichoke hearts, roughly chopped

2 cups peas, cooked

1 large red bell pepper, seeded and small diced

½ cup red onion, minced

2½ ounces parmesan shavings

*Make salad:*

Crumble the crispy bacon and rough chop the eggs. Set both aside in separate bowls. Arrange half the spinach on the bottom of the trifle dish and then add the chopped artichokes. Top with half each of the peas, diced red pepper, and onions, followed by all of the chopped eggs. Sprinkle ½ teaspoon of ground pepper and ½ teaspoon of salt on top of eggs. Add the remaining spinach, peas, red pepper, and onions to the dish in that order.

Remove the dressing from the refrigerator and spread evenly onto top of salad. Garnish with the crumbled bacon and the parmesan cheese.

---

### Layered Dressing

You will need: 1 (17.6-ounce) package Fage yogurt, 2 tablespoons mayonnaise, 2 tablespoons finely chopped dill, 2 teaspoons onion powder, ½ teaspoon salt, ¼ teaspoon ground pepper.

**Directions:**

Whisk together all ingredients in a medium bowl. Place in refrigerator while you prepare the salad.

---

# WARM CASHEW CHICKEN SALAD

*This is a warm, "a la minute" salad perfect for fall brunches. Loaded with edamame, chicken, cashews, and bacon, this salad packs in the protein and showcases different textures, making it filling and unique.*

*Salad:*

- 10 ounces baby spinach
- 10 ounces fresh or frozen edamame, shelled
- 1 cup roasted salted cashews, roughly chopped
- 4 strips oven-baked crispy bacon (recipe on page 159), chopped
- 1½ pounds chicken breast or tenders
- 1 teaspoon salt
- ½ teaspoon ground pepper
- ½ teaspoon onion powder
- 2 tablespoons cornstarch
- 2 tablespoons olive oil

*Make salad:*

Place the spinach, edamame, cashews, and chopped bacon in a large bowl and set aside in refrigerator.

Small dice the chicken and transfer to a medium bowl. Toss them with the salt, pepper, and onion powder. Add the cornstarch and coat well. Heat 2 tablespoons olive oil in a large sauté pan over medium heat. Add the chicken and cook until well done and nicely browned, about 8 minutes. Transfer to the bowl with the spinach mixture.

---

## Dressing

You will need: 2 tablespoons olive oil, ½ cup thinly sliced red onion, 2 tablespoons minced shallot, 2 minced garlic cloves, ⅓ cup red wine vinegar, ⅓ cup Dijon mustard, ⅓ cup honey, salt and pepper.

## Directions:

In the same sauté pan, add the oil and cook the red onions, shallots, and garlic over medium heat for 1 minute. Whisk in the vinegar, mustard, and honey, and let boil for another minute. Season with a little salt and pepper. Pour over the spinach mixture and toss to coat. Serve immediately.

---

# Kale Salad
# with Pecorino, Lemon, and Pine Nuts

Makes 4 servings

½ cup pine nuts

1 lemon

¼ cup extra virgin olive oil

½ teaspoon salt

¼ teaspoon ground pepper

4 ounces Pecorino

1 bunch curly green kale, washed and dried well

*This salad is simple yet oh-so-tasty. Salty pecorino and fruity lemon blend perfectly with the mildly bitter kale and sweet pine nuts. Make sure to chiffonade the kale to make it easier to eat. This salad can sit for hours after dressing without wilting.*

Place a sauté pan over a medium-low heat. Add the pine nuts and give them a good shake to spread them out evenly in the pan. Shake the pan every few seconds to prevent the nuts from burning. When the nuts are fragrant and slightly browned, transfer them to a plate to cool. Set aside.

Finely zest the lemon with a microplane over a large bowl. Add the juice of the lemon, followed by the olive oil, salt, and pepper. Whisk until incorporated. Finely grate the Pecorino with a microplane over the bowl and stir in.

Trim away the kale stems and chiffonade the leaves. Add to the bowl and toss the salad until the kale is evenly coated with the dressing. Let sit for at least 30 minutes in the refrigerator before serving.

# MAC AND CHEESE

MAKES 4 SERVINGS

*The textured layers of creamy cheese, chewy pasta, and crunchy panko topping make this mac and cheese so satisfying. For the sauce, I use a combination of sharp white cheddar and the wonderful semi-soft fontina cheese with its buttery nutty flavor.*

*Make topping:*
In a small sauté pan, melt the butter over medium heat. Stir in the panko and salt. Toast until panko is golden brown, about 2 minutes. Set aside.

*Make casserole:*
Combine the cheese in a large bowl. Separate out ½ cup of the blended cheese mixture for later.

In a 3-quart ovenproof pot (I like to use a Dutch oven), melt the butter over medium heat. Add the flour and stir continuously until tan in color, about 5 minutes.

Combine the milk and cream and warm in microwave. Slowly whisk into the pot along with the bay leaf, mustard, salt, pepper, and nutmeg. Stir occasionally and continue to cook over low heat until thickened, about 10 minutes. Remove from heat and whisk in the cheese in three portions. Cover and set aside. (If you prefer a looser casserole, you can add a little water to the sauce at this point.)

Preheat oven to 350°F. Cook macaroni to al dente according to package directions. Strain them in a colander and stir pasta into the cheese sauce. Top with the reserved cheese mixture, followed by the panko topping. Bake 15 minutes. Top with freshly ground pepper, if desired.

Topping:

1 tablespoon unsalted butter

¼ cup panko bread crumbs

pinch of salt

Casserole:

8 ounces sharp white Cheddar, grated

4 ounces Fontina, grated

4 tablespoons unsalted butter, soft

4 tablespoons all-purpose flour

1 cup whole milk

1 cup heavy cream

1 bay leaf

1 teaspoon ground mustard

1 teaspoon salt

¼ teaspoon black pepper, freshly ground

¼ teaspoon ground nutmeg

½ pound (2 cups) elbow macaroni

# Breakfast Gratin

*I find myself making this robust gratin after the holidays when I have lots of left-over ham in the fridge. It's the epitome of a savory breakfast casserole complete with creamy potatoes, salty ham, and protein-packed eggs. This is my mom's recipe and it's a keeper.*

2 tablespoons unsalted butter, soft
6 large eggs
2 cups half-and-half
1 garlic clove, minced
1 teaspoon salt
½ teaspoon ground pepper
2 pounds (about 6 medium) Yukon gold potatoes
6 ounces smoked ham, brunoised
¼ cup minced red onion
1 cup Italian blend shredded cheese
1 ½ cups sour cream
1 tablespoon all-purpose flour
1 teaspoon paprika

Preheat oven to 350°F. Butter the bottom and sides of a 9 x 13-inch casserole dish and set aside.

Cook the eggs to hard boil stage according to the recipe on page 105. Cut them into ¼-inch-thick slices and set aside.

Combine the half-and-half, garlic, salt, and pepper in a large pot over low heat. Let the mixture slowly warm while you prepare the potatoes.

Wash the potatoes under cold running water with a stiff brush. Dry thoroughly with paper towels. Use a mandoline to cut the potatoes into ⅛-inch-thick slices. Transfer the potatoes to the cream mixture and bring to a simmer. Continue until the potatoes are par-cooked, about 10 minutes. Remove from heat.

Evenly spread one-third of the potato/cream mixture onto the bottom of the prepared pan. Sprinkle half the diced ham over the potatoes, followed by half the eggs and half the onions. Season with salt and pepper. Sprinkle half the cheese on top. Repeat the layering process and end with the last third of the potato/cream mixture.

Stir together the sour cream and flour in a small bowl. Spoon dollops of it on top of the casserole and use a mini offset spatula to spread it thin. Sprinkle the paprika on top. Bake uncovered for 45 minutes. Remove from oven and let rest for 15 minutes before slicing.

*For years, I refused to buy a mandoline, determined to use my knife skills at all times. After finally purchasing one, I realized how my stubbornness needlessly robbed me of pleasure and time. So please, if you don't own one, get one. Making this recipe will easily feel like a joy rather than a chore, I promise.*

*Mixed Berry Sorbet*

# Sweet Endings

After my guests have enjoyed a delicious main course, I always find it worthwhile to give them something sweet to finish the meal. Yes, I realize that most everyone will look at you like you're delusional, thinking they can stomach even one more morsel of food. Nevertheless, it's your role as host to advise them that life is way too short to miss out on the dessert(s) you have painstakingly prepared. Guilt them into it if you must or be prepared to have them take the dessert to-go. They'll certainly thank you later! You'll find a myriad of different desserts in this chapter—from cookies and ice cream to sorbet and pudding—everything you'll need to end your brunch on a delicious note.

# GIANT SUGAR COOKIES

MAKES ABOUT 20 LARGE COOKIES

*These crisp sugar cookies are always a welcome sight. Serve them individually or display a bunch on the table so guests can grab one when they're ready for something sweet.*

Preheat oven to 375°F. Line two sheet trays with parchment or aluminum foil.

In a mixing bowl with the paddle attachment, cream together the butter and sugar on medium speed until light and fluffy, about 2 minutes. Beat in egg and vanilla. Gradually blend in flour, baking soda, and powder.

Fill a small bowl with sugar. Portion the dough with a large ice cream scoop (I use a 1⅓-ounce scoop) directly into the sugar bowl. Coat the ball of dough with sugar, place on prepared sheet tray, and press down slightly with your palm. Continue until all the dough is scooped. Bake 10 to 11 minutes, or until light golden color.

1 cup unsalted butter, soft

1½ cups sugar

1 large egg

2 teaspoons pure vanilla extract

2¾ cups all-purpose flour

1 teaspoon baking soda

½ teaspoon baking powder

sugar, for rolling

# MIXED BERRY SORBET

YIELDS 2–3 SERVINGS

*You'll find numerous pints of this refreshing sorbet in my freezer throughout the summer. Its gorgeous hue and vivid taste make this frozen dessert a perpetual favorite. It makes a great palette cleanser between courses or a sweet ending to any summer brunch.*

Add all the ingredients to a pot and warm over medium heat. Mash the berries with the back of the spatula and stir until the sugar is dissolved. Remove from heat and push mixture through a mesh sieve. Discard pulp and place sorbet juice in refrigerator until well-chilled, about 1 hour. Process in an ice cream maker. Freeze or serve immediately.

2 pounds frozen mixed berries, thawed

⅔ cup sugar

1 teaspoon lemon juice

pinch salt

# Peanut Butter Fudge

1 cup semisweet
chocolate chips

¼ cup whole milk

½ cup unsalted butter

¼ cup sugar

¾ cup chunky peanut
butter

¾ cup graham cracker
crumbs

*I like to keep extra batches of this fudge at the beach house for when unexpected company shows up. It's quick to make and keeps well in the freezer. It also looks great when packaged with ribbon as a take-home favor. You can make this fudge vegan friendly by substituting with dairy-free chocolate, almond milk, and margarine.*

Lightly grease an 8 x 8-inch square pan. Line pan with an 8-inch-wide strip of parchment paper, leaving a 2-inch overhang on opposite ends. Set aside.

In a microwave-safe bowl, heat the chocolate chips and milk in 30-second spurts. Stir until smooth and set aside.

Melt butter in a medium pot over low heat. Add the sugar and stir until dissolved. Off heat, add the peanut butter and graham cracker crumbs and stir well.

Add the chocolate mixture to the pot and stir just until the two mixtures are incorporated. Pour into the prepared pan. Keep in refrigerator at least 4 hours before slicing.

# CHOCOLATE CHUNKIES

MAKES ABOUT 24 COOKIES

5 ounces unsalted butter, soft

½ cup plus 1 tablespoon sugar

½ cup light brown sugar

1 large egg

1 teaspoon pure vanilla extract

2 cups semisweet chocolate chunks

1¼ cups all-purpose flour

⅓ cup cocoa powder

2 tablespoons Café Bustelo ground espresso

½ teaspoon baking soda

¼ teaspoon salt

*If you're a chocolate lover like me, these soft and chewy cookies will blow your mind. While any chocolate brand will work just fine, a higher quality will yield more impressive flavor results. I add a bit of ground espresso to these cookies to give them another layer of flavor and my guests an extra boost.*

Preheat the oven to 350°F. Line two sheet trays with aluminum foil.

In a mixing bowl fitted with the paddle attachment, cream the butter and sugars on medium speed until light and fluffy, about 1 minute. Add the egg and vanilla and mix for 1 minute more. Scrape bowl well. Add the remaining ingredients and mix until incorporated.

Scoop the dough onto the prepared trays (I use a 1-ounce ice cream scoop). Bake for 10 minutes. Remove from oven and let the cookies cool on the trays.

# SALTED CASHEW SCOTCHIES

MAKES ABOUT 24 COOKIES

*Someone once told me that a cashew tastes like a special occasion. Add cashews to any dish and trust me—there won't be a nut left on the plate. These salty sweet cookies have cashews in every bite and keep well for days in an airtight container.*

Preheat oven to 350°F. Line a sheet tray with aluminum foil or parchment and set aside.

In a mixing bowl fitted with the paddle attachment, cream the butter and sugar on medium speed for 2 minutes until light and fluffy. Scrape down bowl and mix in the egg and vanilla. Add flour, ½ cup of the cashews, oats, butterscotch chips, salt, baking soda, and baking powder and beat on low speed until combined.

Finely chop the remaining cashew pieces and spread out on a plate. Using a 1-ounce scoop, portion the dough directly onto the cashew pieces and flatten each piece with your palm to about ½-inch thick. Invert them onto the prepared sheet tray.

Bake for 11 to 12 minutes until tops are lightly browned. Remove from oven and let cool completely before serving.

½ cup unsalted butter, soft

½ cup light brown sugar

1 large egg

1 teaspoon pure vanilla extract

1¼ cups all-purpose flour

1¼ cups salted cashew pieces

½ cup rolled oats

½ cup butterscotch chips

1 teaspoon salt

½ teaspoon baking soda

½ teaspoon baking powder

# SALTED CARAMEL BUTTER BRICKLE ICE CREAM

MAKES 1 QUART

**Butter Brickle:**

¼ cup unsalted butter, soft

¼ cup sugar

1 tablespoon water

pinch of salt

¼ teaspoon pure vanilla extract

**Salted Caramel Ice Cream:**

2 cups whole milk

2 tablespoons unsalted butter, soft

¾ teaspoon sea salt

5 large egg yolks

1¼ cup sugar

1 cup heavy cream

ice bath

*Butter brickle is an easy to make old-fashioned toffee made with common pantry items. In this recipe, the brickle adds a nice soft bite to the smooth ice cream. If you don't care for brickle, you can make the salted caramel ice cream on its own.*

*Make butter brickle (the day before):*
Line a sheet tray with parchment paper or a silpat. In a small pot, cook the butter, sugar, water, and salt over high heat to 298°F. Occasionally stir the mixture to ensure even coloring. Remove pot from heat when temperature is reached and stir in the vanilla. Pour brickle onto the prepared tray and spread as thin as you can with an offset spatula. Set aside to cool overnight.

*Make salted caramel ice cream (the day before):*
Set up a mesh strainer over a bain-marie or stainless steel bowl. Prepare an ice bath. Add 1 cup milk, butter, and sea salt to the bain-marie. In a large bowl, whisk the egg yolks and ¼ cup sugar. Set aside.

In a medium pot over medium heat, cook the remaining 1 cup sugar a little at a time to caramel stage. Remove from heat and carefully stir in the heavy cream. Return to medium heat, add the remaining 1 cup of milk, and cook until sugar is dissolved. Add about ½ cup of the hot mixture to the egg yolks and whisk in. Then add back to the pot and cook until it thickens and coats the back of the spatula. (You don't want the mixture to boil.) Strain into bain-marie or bowl and stir mixture until butter is melted and incorporated. Let sit in ice bath until completely chilled, stirring occasionally. Cover and chill in refrigerator overnight.

*The next day:*
Crush the brickle in a food processor or with a sharp knife. Churn the ice cream base according to ice cream machine directions. Fold in the crushed brickle and let sit in freezer for at least 4 hours before serving.

# Black and Blue Crostata

MAKES ONE 9-INCH CROSTATA

*A nice change from a typical pie, this sweet crostata has a wonderfully soft cookie-like crust with a preserve-like filling. The lattice top is surprisingly easy to create, too.*

**Make crust:**

Using a stand mixer fitted with the paddle attachment, cream the butter and sugar on medium speed until light and fluffy, about 2 minutes. Add the egg and mix for another minute. Add the remaining ingredients and mix just until dough is formed. Shape into two discs, wrap each with plastic wrap, and let chill in refrigerator 30 minutes.

**Make filling:**

Combine the berries, sugar, flour, and water in a large bowl. Melt the butter in a deep sauté pan over medium heat and add the berry mixture. Cook mixture for about 4 minutes, stirring occasionally. Mash a third of the berries with a large spoon. Continue cooking for 3 more minutes until thickened. Transfer to a shallow baking pan and let cool in refrigerator. Stir occasionally to speed up cooling.

**Make crostata:**

Remove one disc of dough from refrigerator and roll out to a 10-inch round between two sheets of parchment or wax paper. Remove top paper and flip dough onto 9-inch pie plate. Trim, leaving a ½-inch overhang, and flip inward. Press dough into the sides such that it is flush with the top of plate. Poke holes into dough with fork and place in refrigerator for 10 minutes.

Crust:

6 ounces unsalted butter, soft

⅓ cup sugar

1 large egg

2¼ cups all-purpose flour

½ teaspoon salt

2 teaspoons finely grated fresh lemon zest

Filling:

16 ounces blueberries

6 ounces blackberries

½ cup sugar

¼ cup all-purpose flour

¼ cup water

2 tablespoons unsalted butter

1 large egg, whisked

sugar for sprinkling

*Continued on page 198*

Remove second disc from refrigerator and roll out to a 10-inch round between two sheets of parchment or wax paper. Remove top paper and cut 10 (1-inch-wide) strips. Slide the paper with the strips onto a sheet tray or large plate and chill for 5 minutes.

Preheat oven to 375°F. Place a baking sheet onto the middle rack. Remove pie shell from refrigerator and fill with the berry mixture (lukewarm is fine). Arrange 5 strips across filling, trim ends flush with crust and press them slightly into the crust. Arrange remaining 5 strips diagonally on top of the other strips. Trims edges flush with crust and again press them slightly into the crust. Brush lattice with whisked egg and generously sprinkle with sugar. Bake for 55 minutes until filling bubbles and crust is golden brown. Let crostata cool completely before cutting.

# Banana Pudding

MAKES 4–6 SERVINGS

*I used to work at a bakery in New York City and for months straight I ate their banana pudding after every shift. I eventually caught a glimpse of the recipe and was shocked to see it was made with instant pudding and cool whip. Since then, I've tried making it with substitutions and it just isn't the same or nearly as delicious. I made one change, though: I added evaporated milk to make the pudding creamier.*

1 (3.4-ounce) package instant vanilla pudding mix

2 cups evaporated milk

1 (8-ounce) package Cool Whip

5–6 ounces vanilla wafers

2 large ripe bananas, sliced into ¼-inch coins

In a large bowl, whisk the pudding mix and evaporated milk for about 2 minutes until thickened. Whisk in the cool whip.

In a 3-quart glass bowl, layer the pudding, wafers, and bananas, ending with the wafers on top for decorative purposes. Cover and chill for at least 4 hours before serving.

# Key Lime Tart with Macadamia Coconut Crust

MAKES ONE 10-INCH TART

*Crust:*

2 cups graham cracker crumbs

½ cup raw macadamia nuts, chopped

⅓ cup sweetened coconut, shredded

⅓ cup sugar

pinch of salt

6 ounces unsalted butter, melted

*Filling:*

1 (14-ounce) can condensed milk

½ cup key lime juice

½ cup sour cream

1 large egg

*Topping:*

2 cups heavy cream, chilled

1 tablespoon sugar

1 teaspoon pure vanilla extract

lime zest, optional

*I love key lime tart because it so vividly tastes like summer to me. Even better, it can be made year round thanks to key lime juice being readily available in grocery stores. In my version, I add macadamia nuts and shredded coconut to the crust to provide texture and bite, making it the perfect complement to the tangy filling and sweet whipped topping.*

*Make crust:*

Preheat oven to 350°F. Grease a 10-inch springform pan and set aside. Combine all the dry ingredients in a large bowl. Add the melted butter and mix well with hands. Pat mixture onto the bottom of the pan. Bake crust for 10 minutes and set aside.

*Make filling:*

Whisk together the milk, juice, sour cream, and egg until combined. Pour into crust and bake for 10 minutes. Place in refrigerator and let cool completely until set, about 2 to 3 hours.

*Make topping:*

In a mixer fitted with the whip attachment, mix the heavy cream, sugar, and vanilla to stiff peak. Remove the tart from the springform pan and transfer to serving plate. Pipe the whipped cream over the filling. Garnish with lime zest, if desired. Keep in refrigerator until serving time.

# Peanut Galette

MAKES ONE 10-INCH GALETTE

*This delicious galette tastes like a super-charged PayDay candy bar. It has a sweet vanilla and caramel layer packed with crunchy peanuts and surrounded by a flaky, buttery crust. It's satisfying on its own or served with vanilla ice cream.*

### Crust:

1¼ cups all-purpose flour

½ teaspoon salt

6 ounces unsalted butter, cold and cubed

¼ cup ice water

*Make crust:*

In a mixing bowl with the paddle attachment, mix the flour and salt. Add the butter cubes and mix on low speed until butter breaks down to pea size. Add the ice water all at once and mix just until dough starts coming together. Form into a disc with lightly floured hands, wrap with plastic, and refrigerate until chilled, about 2 hours.

Coat the bottom and sides of a 10-inch springform pan with nonstick spray. On a lightly floured surface, roll out the dough to a ¼-inch-thick circle, roughly 14 inches in diameter. Drape over the prepared pan and gently press the dough into the bottom and up along the sides. Prick the bottom with a fork. Refrigerate for 15 minutes to chill.

### Peanut Filling:

½ cup corn syrup

¼ cup sugar

1 large egg

2½ tablespoons all-purpose flour

2 teaspoons unsalted butter, melted

2 teaspoons pure vanilla extract

¾ cup roasted salted peanuts

1 tablespoon sugar for sprinkling

*Make peanut filling:*

Preheat oven to 375°F. In a large bowl, whisk together the corn syrup, sugar, egg, flour, butter, and vanilla. Stir in the peanuts and pour filling into the chilled dough. Trim the edges of the dough so they're three-quarters of the way up the sides. It's okay if the sides are not even—you want a rustic look. Gently fold the dough over the filling in an overlapping pattern. Sprinkle 1 tablespoon sugar over the crust. Bake until filling is set and crust is golden brown, about 35 minutes. Let cool completely before serving.

*Sidebar: Don't like peanuts? Try this recipe with walnuts instead.*

★ 203 ★

# Upside Down Plum Cornmeal Cake

## Makes one 9-inch cake

### Caramel Plum:

1 large ripe black or red plum

⅓ cup light brown sugar

¼ cup salted butter, soft

½ teaspoon pure vanilla extract

### Cornmeal Cake:

½ cup all-purpose flour

⅓ cup sugar

¼ cup cornmeal

1 teaspoon baking powder

¼ teaspoon salt

⅓ cup unsalted butter, melted

1 large egg

3 tablespoons whole milk

*This cake pairs well with La Crema 2013 Chardonnay Sonoma Coast.*

*This is my favorite dessert in the book. Plums typically appear in May and extend till August so be sure to try out this recipe at the height of their season. In this yummy upside down cake, the bottom layer of fresh plums roast in a caramel sauce while a tender cornmeal cake bakes above, creating a mouthwatering, warm, buttery dessert you and your guests will devour.*

Preheat oven to 350°F. Grease a 9-inch, shallow glass pie dish with cooking spray and set aside.

*Make caramel plum:*
Slice the plum in half, remove seed, and cut each half into 7 to 8 wedges.

Combine the brown sugar, butter, and vanilla in a small pot and bring to a boil for 30 seconds over high heat. Pour into the pie plate. Carefully lay the plum wedges in the caramel in a concentric circle and then fill in the center. Set aside.

*Make cornmeal cake:*
In a large bowl, whisk together the flour, sugar, cornmeal, baking powder, and salt. Add the butter, egg, and milk, and whisk until incorporated. Slowly pour over the plums and bake until golden brown or when a toothpick inserted in the center comes out clean, about 25 minutes. Remove from oven and let sit for 10 minutes before inverting onto a serving plate.

# LEMON CHESS CHEESECAKE

MAKES ONE 9-INCH CHEESECAKE

*One of my customers shared with me her sister's recipe for Chess Pie, a classic southern dessert. While tasty, it was achingly sweet, as many Southern desserts should be. I tinkered with the recipe to make it to my liking and paired it with cheesecake, creating a luscious, creamy dessert with a delicious lemon bar layer. Try it—you'll love it.*

## Make crust:

Preheat oven to 350°F. Grease a 9 x 2-inch round cake pan and line the bottom and sides with parchment.

Combine graham crumbs and sugar in a small bowl. Stir in the melted butter and press into the bottom and sides of the prepared pan. Let chill in refrigerator.

## Make lemon chess:

In a large bowl, whisk together the sugar and flour. Add in the remaining ingredients until combined and pour into crust. Bake for 25 minutes. Let cool in refrigerator for 10 minutes.

## Make cheesecake:

Place a water bath on the middle rack of the oven. Reduce heat to 325°F.

In a mixing bowl with the paddle attachment, beat cream cheese until smooth. Mix in the sugar on low speed until incorporated. Add the eggs, one at a time, scraping well after each addition. Blend in the sour cream and vanilla. Carefully pour cheesecake batter over lemon layer. Place in the water bath and bake for 80 minutes. Remove from water bath and let cheesecake set up overnight in refrigerator.

Crust:
1½ cups graham cracker crumbs
1 tablespoon sugar
3 ounces unsalted butter, melted

Lemon Chess:
1 cup sugar
½ tablespoon all-purpose flour
2 large eggs
2 tablespoons unsalted butter, melted
2 tablespoons evaporated milk
2 tablespoons lemon juice
1 teaspoon lemon zest

Cheesecake:
8 ounces cream cheese, soft
½ cup sugar
2 large eggs, room temperature
1 cup sour cream
1 teaspoon pure vanilla extract

# Sample Brunch Menus

**Lazy Summer Afternoons**

Infused Water

Honey Oat Bran Muffins

Eggs San Clemente

Mixed Berry Sorbet

**Misty Mornings**

Vanilla Bean French Press Coffee

Blackberry Streusel Coffee Cake

Baked Eggs Milanese

**Formal Gathering**

Classic Mimosa

Croissants

Poached Eggs

Ten Veggie Hash

Key Lime Tart with Macadamia Coconut Crust

**Springtime Showers**

Roasted Beet Bloody Mary

Shrimp N' Grits

Upside Down Plum Cornmeal Cake

**Gal Casual**

Prosecco and Guava Bellini

Easy Apple Turnovers

Breakfast Gratin

Strawberries, Cabernet, and Black Pepper

**Winter Social**

Slow Cooker Mulled Cider

Broiled Grapefruit with Brown Sugar and Tarragon

Warm Cashew Chicken Salad

Peanut Galette

# Acknowledgments

First, I'd like to thank my agent, Deborah Ritchken, who continues to believe that my recipes are important, and who once again has given me the amazing opportunity to write a cookbook. I still can't believe that I'm an author of one cookbook, let alone two.

Throughout the writing of this book, my brain was frequently fried from all the developing, testing, and re-testing of recipes. You can imagine the struggle I went through to actually write something comprehensible after all that. Thankfully, I have a gifted and superbly eloquent editor, Nicole Frail, who makes this book read like a good story and makes me sound like a clever linguist.

There are many people at Skyhorse Publishing who contributed to the success of this book. Thank you to everyone there who worked on this book from start to finish.

People frequently tell me that they buy my cookbooks because of the photos. I used to have mixed emotions about this since it left me feeling like my recipes were all but lost in the mix of gorgeous, eye-catching photos. I'm so grateful to Chau Vuong and Brent Lee for the photographic talents they lent to this project.

I want to extend a special thank-you to all the amazing chefs who taught me when I was a student at the Culinary Institute of America years ago. I was a bright-eyed girl who loved to bake and knew nothing else. They inspired me to take baking seriously and gave me a strong educational foundation that I could build a career on. It's one of the best experiences I've ever had.

Lastly, to the G Crew, thank you for the eggs, hash browns, and quiet conversations that keep me going at work and at play. This one's for you.

# Author Bio

Author and chef Lei Shishak is the owner of Sugar Blossom Bake Shop in the beautiful beachside town of San Clemente, California. Lei began her culinary career in New York City. Upon graduating *magna cum laude* from Bowdoin College, she took an analyst position at the global investment powerhouse JPMorgan in New York City. While climbing the ladder at JPMorgan's Private Bank, she took a weekend job decorating cakes at her neighborhood sweet shop, which quickly sparked her desire to learn more about pastries and baking. To her parents' chagrin, she decided to leave the corporate world and enrolled at the Culinary Institute of America in Hyde Park, New York.

Graduating at the very top of her class with honors and numerous awards, she went on to work in Sun Valley, Idaho, and then in Los Angeles, California. She eventually made her way to Dana Point, California, as the executive pastry chef of Michael Mina's Stonehill Tavern at the AAA Five-Diamond St. Regis Monarch Beach Resort. After more than three years at Stonehill Tavern, she felt the pull to run her own business and decided to open a neighborhood bakery in her favorite beach town of San Clemente in 2010. Thus, Sugar Blossom was born.

Lei has quickly become one of Southern California's most respected bakers, having been honored as the Orange County Pastry Chef of the Year in 2011 by *Riviera Magazine*. At Sugar Blossom, she specializes in custom cakes, cupcakes, cookies, ice cream sandwiches, and her famous cinnamon rolls, using only the highest quality ingredients typically reserved for fine-dining restaurants.

In 2014, she wrote her first cookbook, *Beach House Baking*, heralded by *USA Today* as one of the top 10 cookbooks of summer 2014. She has been featured in *People*, *Riviera Magazine*, *Sunset Magazine*, *Coast Magazine*, the *Los Angeles Daily News*, *Fine Living*, the *Orange County Register*, *KTLA Morning News*, PBS, and many more media outlets.

Lei currently resides in beautiful Dana Point, California. When not in Sugar Blossom's kitchen, she enjoys writing her *Beach Town Baking* blog, promoting her *Slim Bakes* line of all-natural frozen cookie doughs, hiking, and wine tasting.

# Index

# Conversion Charts

## METRIC AND IMPERIAL CONVERSIONS

(These conversions are rounded for convenience)

| Ingredient | Cups/Tablespoons/ Teaspoons | Ounces | Grams/Milliliters |
|---|---|---|---|
| Butter | 1 cup=16 tablespoons= 2 sticks | 8 ounces | 230 grams |
| Cream cheese | 1 tablespoon | 0.5 ounce | 14.5 grams |
| Cheese, shredded | 1 cup | 4 ounces | 110 grams |
| Cornstarch | 1 tablespoon | 0.3 ounce | 8 grams |
| Flour, all-purpose | 1 cup/1 tablespoon | 4.5 ounces/0.3 ounce | 125 grams/8 grams |
| Flour, whole wheat | 1 cup | 4 ounces | 120 grams |
| Fruit, dried | 1 cup | 4 ounces | 120 grams |
| Fruits or veggies, chopped | 1 cup | 5 to 7 ounces | 145 to 200 grams |
| Fruits or veggies, puréed | 1 cup | 8.5 ounces | 245 grams |
| Honey, maple syrup, or corn syrup | 1 tablespoon | .75 ounce | 20 grams |
| Liquids: cream, milk, water, or juice | 1 cup | 8 fluid ounces | 240 milliliters |
| Oats | 1 cup | 5.5 ounces | 150 grams |
| Salt | 1 teaspoon | 0.2 ounces | 6 grams |
| Spices: cinnamon, cloves, ginger, or nutmeg (ground) | 1 teaspoon | 0.2 ounce | 5 milliliters |
| Sugar, brown, firmly packed | 1 cup | 7 ounces | 200 grams |
| Sugar, white | 1 cup/1 tablespoon | 7 ounces/0.5 ounce | 200 grams/12.5 grams |
| Vanilla extract | 1 teaspoon | 0.2 ounce | 4 grams |

# OVEN TEMPERATURES

| Fahrenheit | Celcius | Gas Mark |
|---|---|---|
| 225° | 110° | ¼ |
| 250° | 120° | ½ |
| 275° | 140° | 1 |
| 300° | 150° | 2 |
| 325° | 160° | 3 |
| 350° | 180° | 4 |
| 375° | 190° | 5 |
| 400° | 200° | 6 |
| 425° | 220° | 7 |
| 450° | 230° | 8 |